Healthcare Transformation

A Guide for the
Hospital Board Member

Healthcare Transformation

A Guide for the Hospital Board Member

Maulik S. Joshi, DrPH
Bernard J. Horak, PhD

Foreword by John R. Combes, MD

Health Forum, Inc.
An American Hospital Association Company
CHICAGO

AHA press

CRC Press
Taylor & Francis Group
Boca Raton   London   New York

CRC Press is an imprint of the
Taylor & Francis Group, an **informa** business
A PRODUCTIVITY PRESS BOOK

CRC Press
Taylor & Francis Group
6000 Broken Sound Parkway NW, Suite 300
Boca Raton, FL 33487-2742

© 2009 by Taylor & Francis Group, LLC
CRC Press is an imprint of Taylor & Francis Group, an Informa business

No claim to original U.S. Government works
Printed in the United States of America on acid-free paper
10 9 8 7 6 5 4 3 2 1

International Standard Book Number-13: 978-1-4398-0506-0 (Softcover)

Library of Congress Cataloging-in-Publication Data

Joshi, Maulik.
    Healthcare transformation : a guide for the hospital board member / Maulik S. Joshi and Bernard J. Horak.
        p. ; cm.
    Includes bibliographical references and index.
    ISBN 978-1-4398-0506-0 (pbk. : alk. paper)
    1. Hospital trustees--Handbooks, manuals, etc. I. Horak, Bernard J. II. Title.
    [DNLM: 1. Delivery of Health Care--organization & administration--Handbooks.
2. Quality of Health Care--organization & administration--Handbooks. 3. Governing Board--Handbooks. 4. Hospital Administration--methods--Handbooks. 5. Hospital Administrators--Handbooks. WX 39 J83h 2009]

RA971.J67 2009
362.11068--dc22   2009003730

Visit the Taylor & Francis Web site at
http://www.taylorandfrancis.com

and the CRC Press Web site at
http://www.crcpress.com

Dedication

To our colleagues who provide us constant learning, opportunity, and energy to work toward better healthcare

To our families for all the support and love—Emilie, Ella, and Lucas; Nancy, Rachel, David, Molly, and Willie

Table of Contents

Foreword

It is becoming clearer that the primary fiduciary role of boards is to ensure that their organization delivers safe, effective care that meets the patients' need for a quality of life that is free from suffering and debility. Because board members have a legal duty to act on behalf of the organization's stakeholders and principal among these stakeholders are patients and communities, it is evident that their concerns, intimately related to their health and lives, should be primary. With this deeper understanding that patients and communities have entrusted their health and lives to the healthcare organization comes a change in perspective. The board's principal duty is not to the organization's well-being alone but rather to the well-being of the patients and communities that they serve. To accomplish this reorientation, it will take nothing less than transformative change, moving organizational and practitioners' needs from the center of attention and placing instead the needs and concerns of patients and communities at the center. Boards must lead this reorientation process.

Are boards prepared to take on such a task? The evidence is mixed. There are some great boards setting the quality agenda for their organization, but other boards that are still satisfied with leaving the responsibility for clinical care and quality with the medical staff. In fact, many trustees can be overwhelmed by the complexity of clinical care, the need for expert knowledge, and the presence of those experts in the board room. This can often lead to trustees avoiding their responsibility to ask the right questions, challenge conventional thinking, and use the organization mission to provide clarity to their decision-making. Only recently have new tools become available to help boards meet these obligations and challenges.

Over the past year, as part of its "5 Million Lives" campaign, the Institute for Healthcare Improvement has focused on engaging boards on quality through education, consensus recommendations, and identification of leading practices. The American Hospital Association's Center for Healthcare Governance (Center) with support from the Massachusetts Hospital Association and Blue Cross/Blue Shield of Massachusetts has developed a trustee quality curriculum that is being delivered in board rooms around the country. The object is to engage the board in a dialogue on how they can exercise the responsibility for quality by practicing good governance principles. Additionally, the Center is publishing its second Blue Ribbon Panel report on trustee core competencies, among which are information seeking (asking the right questions), innovative thinking (looking at issues in new ways), and leadership for change (defining the vision for change). With all of this education and research activity, there is even a greater need for practical resources to aid boards in their leadership role of transforming healthcare. With *Healthcare Transformation: A Guide for the Hospital Board Member*, Maulik Joshi and Bernard Horak have successfully met that need.

This volume concisely presents the ten major transformers for healthcare in the first part of the twenty-first century and how boards can understand and use them to transform their own organizations. By outlining the challenges, illustrating the transformational process, identifying the current best practice, and, most importantly, articulating the critical questions board members should ask, this book makes an important and invaluable contribution to elevating board performance in quality and safety. It also assists in developing the necessary trustee competencies to garner organizational success. Practical information is provided in each chapter, which helps demystify the healthcare environment and provide direction to boards as they navigate their own and their organization's course through the ever changing challenges and obstacles in healthcare.

The new frontier for improving board performance lies not in the structure of the board or in its written policies and procedures but rather in its board room culture and the individual and collective behaviors of its members. This guide can help boards develop that culture, one of respectful inquisitiveness based on a clear understanding of the forces that are shaping healthcare. By placing boards in a stronger position to lead, healthcare organizations will be better able to draw on their trustees' perspective and experience. This book will aid your board in achieving that stronger position and in turn help your organization perform more successfully in the new healthcare world.

As you refer to this guide as either as a trustee, an executive, or as a student of healthcare governance, consider how this approach to transformation can lead us back once again to that strong bond of trust with our patients and communities. Focus on how we can raise the board culture to make our organizations better through their effective challenging of our current performance. Strengthening the trustees' role in helping our healthcare institutions fulfill the promises made to our patients and communities has never been more important. This book is your guide.

John R. Combes, MD
President and Chief Operating Officer
Center for Healthcare Governance

Preface

Today's healthcare is unlike yesterday's and unlike tomorrow's. Healthcare is in the midst of dramatic, needed change. Healthcare delivery, financing, and resourcing have seen significant alterations over the last few decades. However, the transformation ahead will surpass any changes to date. Our healthcare system is unable to continue as is, and healthcare transformation, or the fundamental change in form and function, will be led by you—healthcare executives and board members.

The purpose of this book is to provide hospital board members and executives with a practical guide for their role and an opportunity to be not only literate in healthcare quality, but also supportive and engaged in the transformation of their organization and the industry to better health.

This book is not about board committee structures and charters, agenda setting, and legal fiduciary aspects of being a board member in today's climate. Wonderful resources currently exist on those topics. This book is about how the healthcare industry is transforming and how you, as a board member, will be knowledgeable and skillful in leading this charge. The book is designed to be succinct, informative, and actionable by providing you the background, the opportunity, and the questions to ask and discuss.

Our aim was to keep the guide concise so that all board members can become fairly literate on the major issues in healthcare for the future. This book is ideal for orienting new board members and for providing more experienced board members with a knowledge base and questions to facilitate engagement on these important issues.

We greatly encourage you to read and reread this book as well as to refer to the questions that a board member should ask (compiled in the appendix). We hope this collection of important questions will be used by your board and leadership on an ongoing basis to critically question the hospital's progress toward transformation.

The format of this book is straightforward. After the introductory chapter, there are ten chapters that articulate each of the ten healthcare transformers. Each of those ten chapters is organized by:

- The problem: A brief, quantitative look at the problem.
- The transformer: What will transform and make healthcare different.
- Best practices: Examples of current best practices indicative of the transformer.
- Board questions: Questions every board member should consider asking and every healthcare executive should ask and be prepared to answer.

The concluding chapter provides the overall governance engagement checklist—the things to do to make sure you and your governance and senior leader colleagues are on the track to being engaged and leading your organization's transformation. Finally, the appendix compiles the board questions from each chapter as an easy-to-use reference for the questions that should be posed at board meetings.

Of course, we are very interested in your feedback. Your comments as to how we could make this book better would be greatly appreciated. Please feel free to e-mail us at:

Maulik S. Joshi   mjoshi@aha.org
Bernard J. Horak   bhorak@aol.com

1

Introduction

CURRENT CHALLENGES IN HEALTHCARE QUALITY

The quality of healthcare in the United States is of national concern. A wake-up call for health system change was provided by the Institute of Medicine (IOM) in its landmark report, *To Err Is Human: Building a Safer Health System* (2000), which estimated that between 44,000 and 98,000 people die each year because of medical error. In a follow-up report, the IOM stated:

> The American healthcare delivery system is in need of fundamental change. Many patients, doctors, nurses, and healthcare leaders are concerned that the care delivered is not, essentially, the care we should receive. The frustration levels of both patients and clinicians have probably never been higher. Yet the problems remain. Healthcare today too frequently harms and routinely fails to deliver its potential benefits....Quality problems are everywhere, affecting many patients. Between the healthcare we have and the care we should receive lies not just a gap, but a chasm. (IOM 2001)

Major challenges in healthcare quality are affecting patients, families, and providers and resulting in poor clinical outcomes. The United States ranks last out of the industrialized countries on preventable mortality. For 37 core indicators of performance, the United States attains an overall score of 65 out of a possible 100 when comparing national averages with U.S. and international benchmarks. These poor outcomes occur despite the United States spending 16% of its gross national product (GNP) on healthcare—a percentage larger than any other country (CMS 2008). U.S. health insurance administrative costs are 30–70% higher than in countries with mixed private/public insurance systems (Commonwealth Fund 2008). In addition, more than 5% of healthcare expenditures are a result of fraud and abuse, such as billing for services not rendered or inaccurate coding and billing (Ingenix 2004).

There are also several national health policy concerns, including large variations of care in different geographic regions. The Dartmouth Atlas reports that the amount of care provided to patients with similar diagnoses, in terms of physician visits, treatment interventions, and medications, varies up to 30% across regions in the United States (Wennberg et al. 2006). Currently, 15% of Americans are uninsured, with a total of 75 million working-age adults (42%) either uninsured or underinsured, a sharp increase from 61 million (35%) in 2003. Minorities, low-income, or uninsured adults and children are more likely to wait when sick; encounter delays and poorly coordinated care; and have untreated chronic diseases, avoidable hospitalizations, and worse outcomes. Technology (clinical information systems) could address many efficiency and quality concerns. However, only 28% of primary care physicians use electronic medical records (EMRs), lagging far behind leading countries where nearly all physicians use EMRs (Commonwealth Fund 2008). These numbers and trends continue to change but often in the wrong direction for the United States.

Some advances are taking place, including the government's pay-for-performance (P4P) efforts in the Medicare program to incentivize providers for good outcomes. Also, advances have been seen in the science of quality improvement, particularly with respect to best practices to address patient safety issues as will be identified in this book. Clearly, board and executive leadership are needed to guide change to improve systems of care at each hospital or healthcare organization. This need can be also seen in the following data:

- Less than 50% of adults are able to get a timely appointment with a physician, and 73% report much difficulty in obtaining care after hours (Commonwealth Fund 2008).
- Eighteen percent of patients are readmitted, showing a lack of adequate care while hospitalized (Commonwealth Fund 2008).
- Eighteen percent of working adults state that they are unable to work or carry out everyday activities because of health problems, usually because of a lack of prevention or ineffective management of chronic care diseases (Commonwealth Fund 2008).
- Only 54.9% of patients receive recommended care (McGlynn et al. 2003).

- Only 67% of patients would definitely recommend the hospital in which they received care (Jha et al. 2008).

YOUR DUTY

As a board member, you have a fiduciary role in the performance of the hospital. You have several accountabilities and duties in carrying out your governance role. Most important is to ensure that the mission of the organization is achieved. In some form, each hospital has a mission that addresses community health improvement, quality and safety of patient care, customer/patient satisfaction, community benefit, and financial sustainability. Additionally, boards must continually respond to new clinical, operational, and regulatory developments associated with quality of care.

Board obligations with respect to quality of care arise in two different areas:

1. The decision-making function: The application of duty of care to a specific decision or particular board action (e.g., granting, restricting, or revoking privileges of members of the medical staff).

2. The oversight function: The application of duty of care with respect to overseeing operations (e.g., assuring that a reasonable quality information and medical error-reporting system exists) (Callender et al. 2007).

The problems identified earlier are related to the oversight function—the obligation you have as a board member to "keep a finger on the pulse" of the activities of the organization in addressing these and other quality issues. With respect to the oversight function, a joint publication from the U.S. Department of Health and Human Services and the American Health Lawyers Association (AHLA) states:

> The basic governance obligation to guide and support executive leadership in the maintenance of quality of care and patient safety is an ongoing task. Board members are increasingly expected to assess organizational performance on emerging quality of care concepts and arrangements as they implicate issues of patient safety, appropriate levels of care, cost reduction, reimbursement, and collaboration among providers and practitioners. These are all components of the oversight function. (Callender et al. 2007, 4)

NEED FOR TRANSFORMATIONAL CHANGE AND LEADERSHIP

Improving the health of your community is basically the fundamental mission of almost every healthcare organization. To fulfill that mission and to address the issues identified earlier, we need to transform healthcare. Hence, this guide is about what you need to do to support the transformation of your hospital to ensure quality and patient safety.

Incremental improvement is not enough to deal with long-standing quality issues. Incrementalism is too slow and will not address deep systems issues in healthcare. What is needed is transformational leadership that: (1) alters the culture of the institution by changing select underlying assumptions and institutional behaviors, processes, and products; (2) is deep and pervasive, affecting the whole institution; (3) is intentional; and (4) occurs over time (Eckel, Hill, and Green 1998).

THE TOP TEN HEALTHCARE TRANSFORMERS

The model in Figure 1.1 is to guide the transformation in your organization. As you see, there are ten healthcare transformers. A book chapter is devoted to each transformer. Key aspects of each transformer are highlighted below:

Transformer 10: Reliably Implement the Tried and True (Chapter 2)

This transformer is about reliably implementing known best practices. The tried and true represent healthcare processes in which the evidence is strong for the best practice. These processes have been studied, documented, and proven to be effective in improving the health of patients. This transformer is not about the next great idea but how to consistently implement at a high-performance level practices that have been researched and for which the evidence has been known for years. A transformed healthcare system will require the consistent implementation of these best practices.

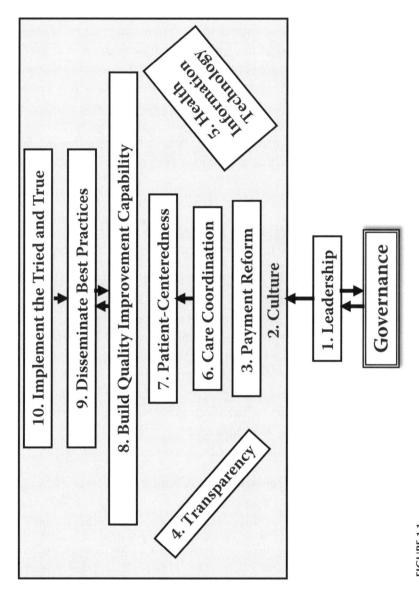

FIGURE 1.1
Top Ten Healthcare Transformers.

Transformer 9: Disseminate Best Practices (Chapter 3)

This transformer is about being effective and efficient in disseminating best practices and improvements throughout the health system. Whether it is called knowledge transfer, translating research into practice, spreading improvement, diffusion of innovations, or disseminating best practices, the process and structure of taking something that works well from one part of the system to the rest of the system is no easy task, nor does it happen organically. A dissemination plan must be in place to effectively spread best practices throughout a health system. As compelling as best practices or improvement results may be, they will not easily transfer to other areas without a formal plan that is designed and monitored to ensure success.

Transformer 8: Build Organizational Quality Improvement Capability (Chapter 4)

This transformer is borrowed from other industries in which the capability of an organization for improvement is essential. To successfully implement this transformer, organizations must (1) promulgate their quality improvement vision and approach (goals and philosophy); (2) define the key quality improvement knowledge and skills needed by the organization; (3) establish a comprehensive development program for all executives, managers, team leaders, and employees, particularly those who come into direct contact with patients/customers; and (4) continually learn from new best practices and their own experiences.

Transformer 7: Patient-Centeredness (Chapter 5)

There are multiple definitions and concepts of patient-centeredness, which has also been characterized as person-centered, family-centered, relationship-centered, consumer-focused, and consumer-directed. Organizations must systematically implement policies, programs, and a culture that will address the multiple aspects of patient-centeredness, including respect for patients' preferences, needs, and values; importance of patients' emotional needs and physical and emotional comfort; and shared decision-making as an approach to patient and family engagement.

Transformer 6: Care Coordination (Chapter 6)

Coordinating care across services within your hospital (e.g., diagnostic imaging and patient units), across settings (e.g., between the intensive care unit and the medicine floor), or across people (e.g., between your primary care providers and specialists) is a challenge no matter who or where you are. Although we talk about "seamless care," the healthcare industry has failed miserably in achieving it. Care coordination is often recognized as a main driver for poor quality and medical error. To address care coordination, organizations should consider the use of care coordinators (e.g., hospitalists and case managers), joint patient care rounds (i.e., among physicians, nurses, and other providers), team building and interdisciplinary problem-solving meetings, structured communication tools to ensure a good hand-off for patients and patient information, briefings prior to any procedure, and systems that (1) track patients across providers, settings, and time; and (2) send reminders for needed follow-up for exams, tests, and procedures.

Transformer 5: Health Information Technology (Chapter 7)

The promise of the impact of health information technology (HIT) on better health and healthcare is profound. Although there are a vast number of HIT systems (e.g., picture archiving and communication systems, laboratory ordering and results tracking, clinical data repository, dictation, master patient indexing, operating room scheduling, electronic prescribing, and barcode medication administration), three HIT programs that will play a substantial role in healthcare transformation are:

1. Computerized prescriber order entry (CPOE),
2. Electronic health records (EHRs), and
3. Personalized health records (PHRs).

Transformer 4: Transparency (Chapter 8)

More public reporting of quality information is a major trend today in healthcare—how is your hospital responding? Transparency has been, and will continue to be, a transformative factor in our healthcare system. Chapter 8 provides examples of public reporting that have increased organizational quality improvement efforts and looks at how consumers, to a much lesser extent, are using data for decision-making and discussion with their providers. The leadership message from this transformer is to embrace transparency as a change agent and to use it in your own work— whether it is to be transparent regarding your organization's employee satisfaction survey results, quality outcomes, ethics policies, or conflicts of interest. Without transparency, it is difficult for your community to make informed decisions about healthcare. Hence, it is critical that you be transparent with your own data internally and externally, including placing data on patient satisfaction and quality outcomes on your hospital website.

Transformer 3: Payment Reform (Chapter 9)

A growing number of programs in the United States are testing different payment systems. Many of these are pay for performance (P4P) programs, reflecting the linkage of payment to performance levels. Designing, implementing, and learning from P4P and other payment reform programs are instrumental to fundamentally changing the vast and increasing financial facet of healthcare. Reforming the payment system is not a panacea to improved healthcare; however, it is necessary. The healthcare leader's efforts for payment reform should include four major elements:

1. Assess the current payment system and identify areas where the incentives are misaligned.
2. Evaluate the impact of new payment models on the organization's bottom line.
3. Design and test new payment schemes.
4. Learn from these systems.

Transformer 2: Culture (Chapter 10)

Culture is the most often spoken barrier to improving healthcare and yet perhaps the least understood. Culture is the way things are done in an organization and is reflective of behaviors, norms, and beliefs. To create a positive culture that will enhance quality and patient safety, leaders should:

- Make quality and patient safety strategic imperatives.
- Promulgate values of openness of information, a learning organization, and a "no-blame culture."

- Institute policies, systems, and procedures to ensure quick and accurate reporting and discussion of medical errors.
- Conduct team-building to ensure interdisciplinary collaboration, mutual respect, and effective problem-solving of patient care issues.

Transformer 1: Leadership (Chapter 11)

Leadership is the key to organizational performance. Leaders must use proven approaches and take action to ensure high quality of care and patient safety. In its healthcare criteria for performance excellence, the Baldrige National Quality Program identifies leadership as its first criterion and states that leaders should set organizational vision and values, create a sustainable organization, and promote a culture of patient safety. As mentioned, it is critical that leaders institute what is called *transformational change*, that is, changes in values and patterns of behavior so that healthcare organizations address long-standing performance and quality issues. An excellent framework to follow is IHI's Reinersten's model of transformational leadership, which consists of the five interrelated activities of:

1. Setting direction (e.g., having a clear mission, vision, and strategy)
2. Establishing a foundation (e.g., developing future leaders)
3. Building will (e.g., defining the business case for quality)
4. Generating ideas (e.g., benchmarking to find best practices)
5. Executing change (e.g., making quality a line responsibility) (Ransom et al. 2008)

ORGANIZATION OF THE BOOK

The format of this book is straightforward. A chapter is devoted to each of the ten healthcare transformers. As mentioned in the preface, the chapters are organized by:

- The problem: A brief, quantitative look at the problem.
- The transformer: What will transform and make healthcare different.
- Best practices: Examples of current best practices indicative of the transformer.

- Board questions: Questions every board member should consider asking and every healthcare executive should ask and be prepared to answer.

The concluding chapter provides the overall governance checklist—steps to take to ensure you and your governance and senior leader colleagues are engaged in leading your organization's transformation. Finally, the appendix compiles the board questions for each chapter as an easy-to-use reference for discussion at board meetings.

REFERENCES

Callender, A. N., D. A. Hastings, M. C. Hemsley, L. Morris, and M. W. Peregrine. *Corporate Responsibility and Health Care Quality: A Resource for Health Care Boards of Directors.* U.S. Department Health and Human Services and American Health Lawyers Association, 2007, http://www.oig.hhs.gov/fraud/docs/complianceguidance/CorporateResponsibilityFinal%209-4-07.pdf (accessed November 10, 2008).

Clancy, C. C. "Putting Reliability into Practice: Lessons from Healthcare Leaders." *Patient Saf Qual Healthc* 5 (2008): 6–7.

CMS (Centers for Medicare & Medicaid Services). *National Health Expenditure Fact Sheet.* 2008, http://www.cms.hhs.gov/NationalHealthExpendData/25_NHE_Fact_Sheet.asp#TopOfPage (accessed November 18, 2008).

The Commonwealth Fund. *Why Not the Best? National Scorecard on U.S. Health System Performance, 2008.* 2008, http://www.commonwealthfund.org/publications/publications_show.htm?doc_id=692682#areaCitation (accessed November 10, 2008).

Eckel, P., B. Hill, and M. Green. *On Change: En Route to Transformation.* American Council on Education, 1998, http://www.acenet.edu/bookstore/pdf/on-change/on-change1.pdf (accessed November 10, 2008).

Ingenix. "Healthcare Fraud and Abuse Remains a Costly Challenge." *Manag Care Exec* October 1, 2004.

Institute of Medicine Committee on Quality of Health Care in America. *To Err is Human: Building a Safer Health System.* Washington, DC: National Academy Press, 2000.

Institute of Medicine Committee on Quality of Health Care in America. *Crossing the Quality Chasm: A New Health System for the 21st Century.* Washington, DC: National Academy Press, 2001.

Jha, A. K., E. J. Orav, J. Zheng, and A. M. Epstein. "Patients' Perception of Hospital Care in the United States." *N Engl J Med* 359 (2008): 1921–1931.

McGlynn, E. A., S. M. Asch, J. Adams, J. Keesey, J. Hicks, A. DeCristofaro, and E. A. Kerr. "The Quality of Health Care Delivered to Adults in the United States." *N Engl J Med* 348 (2003): 2635–2645.

Ransom, E., M. Joshi, D. Nash, and S. Ransom. *The Healthcare Quality Book*, 2nd ed. Chicago: Health Administration Press, 2008.

Wennberg, J. E., E. S. Fisher, S. M. Sharp, M. McAndrew, and K. K. Bronner. *The Care of Patients with Severe Chronic Illness: A Report on the Medicare Program by the Dartmouth Atlas Project.* Hanover, NH: The Trustees of Dartmouth College, 2006.

2

Healthcare Transformer 10: Reliably Implement the Tried and True

Healthcare Transformer 10 (see Figure 2.1) has little to do with innovation in terms of new medical science. Rather, this transformer is about reliably implementing tried-and-true, known best practices. If you accept tried and true to mean "tested and proved to be worthy," there are dozens of healthcare practices that are tried and true, but not consistently done for every patient every day in the American healthcare system.

The gap between current healthcare and the best care is significant and persistent, so that achieving higher levels of performance is not a trivial

FIGURE 2.1
Top Ten Healthcare Transformers.

matter. Often, individuals and organizations are seeking the new idea. However, this transformer is not about the next great idea, but how we can consistently implement, at a high-performance level, practices that have been researched and for which the evidence has been known for years. A transformed healthcare system will require the consistent implementation of best practices.

PROBLEM

Consider the following data:

- 83%: This is the national average for the percentage of surgery patients (for certain surgeries) who received preventative antibiotic(s) 1 hour before incision. Research shows that surgery patients who get antibiotics within the hour before their operation are less likely to get wound infections. Getting an antibiotic earlier, or after surgery begins, is not as effective. In other words, one of six surgery patients does not get the antibiotic at the right time (U.S. Department of Health & Human Services 2008).
- 68%: This is the national average for the percentage of heart failure patients who were given discharge instructions. Before a heart failure patient leaves the hospital, the hospital staff should provide the following information to help the patient manage symptoms at home: activity level (what the patient can and cannot do), diet (what the patient should and should not eat or drink), medications, follow-up appointment, watching daily weight, and what to do if symptoms worsen. In other words, about one of three heart failure patients does not get complete hospital discharge instructions to help with care at home (U.S. Department of Health & Human Services 2008).
- 12%: This is the national percentage of sick adult patients who waited 4 hours or longer to be seen in the emergency room. In other words, 1 of 8 patients who went to the emergency room waited at least 4 hours before being seen (McCarthy and Leatherman 2006).
- 80,000: This is approximately the number of patients in intensive care units (ICUs) who get a central venous catheter infection each year. Catheter-related bloodstream infections are preventable, can

lead to complications and death, and have an attributable cost in the range of \$30,000–50,000 for each case (Soufir et al. 1999). In other words, in an average hospital, at least 15 ICU patients a year will get a bloodstream infection.

- 7–10%: This is the national average of the percentage of patients who acquire a pressure ulcer (bedsore) while in the hospital. Most hospital-acquired pressure ulcers are preventable, and it costs an average hospital approximately \$500,000 a year to treat pressure ulcers (Courtney, Ruppman, and Cooper 2006). In other words, about 1 of 12 hospitalized patients gets a pressure ulcer.

The above data are merely a sample of many data points. These data may be extrapolated to hospitals throughout the world and to all settings of care—from the nursing home to the doctor's office. These data, however, share several common features:

- They represent healthcare processes in which the evidence is strong for the best practice. These processes have been studied, documented, and proven to be effective in improving the health of patients.
- The results are far from 100%. Although 100% may be a theoretical goal and difficult to achieve, even if one considers 99% or 95% as the goal, these results are a stark deviation from the best.
- There are examples of organizations that have consistently achieved the best practices. The best ways to achieve high-performance levels are portable and achievable.
- The benefits of improving these types of healthcare processes include financial savings and human savings in the form of reduced cost, reduced complications, reduced deaths, better quality of life, and greater patient and provider satisfaction.

Dr. Ken Kizer, former president and chief executive officer of the National Quality Forum and former Undersecretary for Health in the U.S. Department of Veterans Affairs, stated:

> If we would systematically apply what we currently know about quality management to healthcare, it has the potential to save more lives and otherwise improve health more than any foreseeable technological or scientific breakthrough of the next 20 years, including finding cures for diabetes, heart disease, or cancer. ("The Face of Quality" 2005)

TRANSFORMER

The transformative opportunity to reliably implement tried-and-true practices is multifold and includes:

1. Measurable aims: It is critical for improvement to have clear, measurable aims and goals that specifically include the measures to be tracked, the goals to be achieved, and the dates for meeting goals. The aims provide the milestones to work toward.
2. Results tracking: Constant surveillance of key healthcare process results should take place at the management and governance levels. Key results should be reviewed at least quarterly and actionable so that one can assess the impact of a test of change.
3. Project review: Senior leadership should establish a system for ongoing review of key quality improvement initiatives. Assessment should include progress made as well as how barriers can be removed and enablers created.
4. Implementation: Effectively implementing interventions is a challenge in every hospital. Implementation includes many types of interventions that need to be delivered in multiple ways.

One set of interventions includes training and education. Continuous training and education of all staff and providers on current and emerging best practices is essential, whether as a formal program or just-in-time training. Incentives, financial and nonfinancial, can also play a role in encouraging and rewarding improvement. The evidence is clear that incentives for staff and clinicians on performance improvement accelerate improvement. Finally, there exists a core of high-reliability concepts, and the implementation of these concepts yields better performance. High-reliability concepts include being sensitive to operations, reluctant to simplify explanations to problems, preoccupied with failure, resilient to quickly respond to errors, and deferring to frontline expertise (Agency for Healthcare Research and Quality 2008).

Specific to the last point, several interventions are available that can make processes more reliable. The interventions include education, training, developing and using standardized protocols, checklists, and bundles of care.

BEST PRACTICES

There are numerous examples of best practices for the previously mentioned and other important clinical areas. These best practices are found in every type of hospital—small and large, teaching and non-teaching, and urban and rural.

Interventions that can dramatically improve the quality of healthcare include:

- Standing orders and clinical guidelines: Standing orders are a course of treatments and tests that each patient with a given diagnosis receives unless a physician believes there is a compelling reason to change or augment the order. Each instruction requires staff members treating the patient to document what action they took, including any decision not to follow the recommendations. Clinical guidelines are similar in that they are standardized approaches to treating conditions for which the evidence is clear for the best approach.
- Checklists: As simple as it sounds, using a checklist to ensure that all of a patient's individual care practices have been completed has proven to be incredibly effective for healthcare improvement. Checklists are simple in form, serve as a prompt and effective reminder, require less reliance on memory, and can be put into practice efficiently. For example, a checklist to prevent bloodstream infections would include: perform standard hand disinfection before any procedure, wear mask, use a sterile gown and gloves, and prepare the site with a chlorhexidine stick.
- Care bundles: Care bundles are groupings of best practices with respect to a disease process that individually improve care, but when applied together result in substantially greater improvement. The science supporting the bundle components is considered the standard of care.

As an example, Cape Coral Hospital/Lee Memorial Health System in Florida set out to improve care in the ICU by reducing complications and infections from ventilators and central lines (Cape Coral Hospital/Lee Memorial Health System 2008). We can track the hospital's work using the elements from the transformer.

Measurable Aims

Specific project aims include:

- Eliminating ventilator-associated pneumonia (VAP) as evidenced by 1 year or more between episodes by August 2008
- Decreasing incidence of central line-associated bloodstream infections as evidenced by 1 year or more between infections by August 2008

Results Tracking

The following measures were tracked and reported to the team and management:

- Ventilator bundle compliance
- VAP infection rate per 1,000 ventilator days
- Central line bundle compliance
- Central-line-associated bloodstream infection rate per 1,000 central line days

Project Review

The team and leadership routinely reviewed project progress using the above-mentioned measures and goals to identify opportunities for improvement and remove barriers.

Implementation

Cape Coral Hospital/Lee Memorial Health System joined a learning community sponsored by the Institute for Healthcare Improvement (IHI) that allowed the hospital to learn best practices and share stories and lessons with other hospitals working in the same area. Cape Coral Hospital/Lee Memorial Health System's changes included:

- Establishing daily goals to enhance team communication
- Instituting multidisciplinary rounds so all providers review patients together as a team

- Improving communication, especially at transitions by "scripted" shift-to-shift report and multidisciplinary rounds to ensure communication of daily goals and other key content and ensure input from each discipline
- Utilizing "check-out list" to ensure removal of ICU devices and transfer of information to the next level of care
- Using chalkboard to convey daily goals to families and allow them to share questions and concerns
- Establishing reliable processes including the consistent use of the ventilator bundle and central line bundle
- Introducing aggressive hand washing campaign, which increased compliance from 40% to 90%
- Providing waterless soap and disinfectant wipes in multiple convenient locations

Figures 2.2 and 2.3 demonstrate the significant improvement in Cape Coral Hospital/Lee Memorial Health System's desired measures. Figure 2.2 shows that the hospital has gone more than 15 months without a VAP

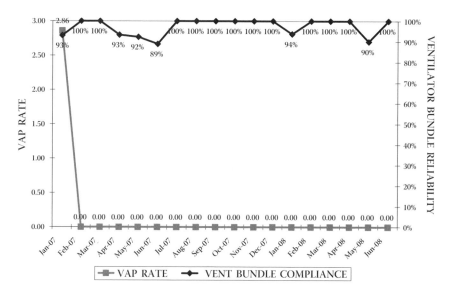

FIGURE 2.2
CCH ICU ventilator bundle/VAP rate.

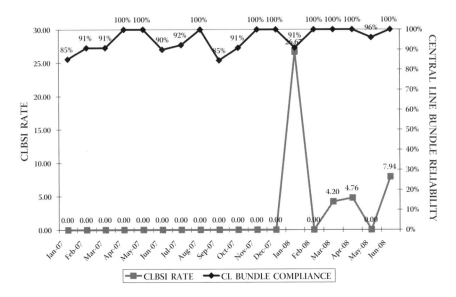

FIGURE 2.3
CCH ICU central line bundle/CLBSI rate.

in its ICU. Figure 2.3 indicates that Cape Coral Hospital/Lee Memorial Health System has maintained a low central line bloodstream infection rate.

BOARD QUESTIONS

As a hospital board member, consider these questions:

1. How are we doing in implementing tried-and-true best practices? What are our results?
2. Have we implemented tried-and-true best practices of standing orders, clinical guidelines, and care bundles?
3. How do our results compare to (state and national) averages and to benchmarks?
4. Have we learned from the best-performing organizations that have achieved benchmark performance?

5. What do we still need to do to address any gaps between our current performance and the best?
6. What are the major lessons (successes and failures) from our recent quality improvement initiatives?
7. Have we "hardwired" (institutionalized and formalized) our processes for consistency and reliability?
8. Do we have the right systems and measures in place to track the sustaining of improved performance?
9. What are the nationally emerging best practices that we should be investigating and implementing?

REFERENCES

Agency for Healthcare Research and Quality (AHRQ). *Becoming a High-Reliability Organization: Operational Advice for Hospital Leaders.* AHRQ Publication No. 08-0022. Rockville, MD: AHRQ, 2008, http://www.ahrq.gov/qual/hroadvice/ (accessed March 6, 2009).

Cape Coral Hospital/Lee Memorial Health System. IHI Improvement Report. *Improving ICU Care: Reducing Complications from Ventilators and Central Lines.* 2008, http://www.ihi.org/IHI/Topics/CriticalCare/IntensiveCare/ImprovementStories/ImprovingICUCareReducingComplicationsfromVentilatorsandCentralLines.htm (accessed September 18, 2008).

Courtney, B., J. Ruppman, and H. Cooper. "Save Our Skin: Initiative Cuts Pressure Ulcer Incidence in Half." *Nurs Manage* 37, no. 4 (2006): 36–45.

"The Face of Quality." *Quality Progress* January 22, 2005.

McCarthy, D., and S. Leatherman. *Performance Snapshots.* The Commonwealth Fund, 2006, http://www.cmwf.org/snapshots (accessed September 2, 2008).

Soufir, L., J. F. Timsit, C. Mahe, J. Carlet, B. Regnier, and S. Chevret. "Attributable Morbidity and Mortality of Catheter-Related Septicemia in Critically Ill Patients: A Matched, Risk-Adjusted, Cohort Study." *Infect Control Hosp Epidemiol* 20, no. 6 (1999): 396–401.

U.S. Department of Health & Human Services. *Hospital Compare.* 2008, http://www.hospitalcompare.hhs.gov (accessed September 2, 2008).

3

Healthcare Transformer 9: Disseminate Best Practices

As noted in the previous chapter, improving healthcare by implementing tried-and-true interventions is a challenge. Although the pace of improvement is slow, there are an increasing number of successful improvement projects, new knowledge discovered, and better practices identified.

However, as we find better ways to deliver healthcare, another challenge arises—how do you "spread," or disseminate, known best practices, innovations, or successful improvement changes from one area of your hospital system to other parts of the hospital system? Whether it is called knowledge transfer, translating research into practice, spreading improvement, diffusion of innovations, or disseminating best practices, the process and structure of taking something that works well from one part of the system to the rest of the system is no easy task, and it does not happen organically.

Healthcare Transformer 9 (see Figure 3.1) is about being effective and efficient in disseminating best practices and improvements throughout the health system.

PROBLEM

The ability to transfer research into practice or to disseminate a best practice is a prevalent problem in many industries. A classic example of the extensive time it takes to disseminate a best practice dates back several hundred years to the British Navy's fight against scurvy, a disease caused by the deficiency of vitamin C (Berwick 2003). Death from scurvy today is rare, but the death toll from scurvy during the early exploration years was significant. A brief history of the attempts to prevent scurvy shed light on the difficulty of spreading knowledge and a better practice.

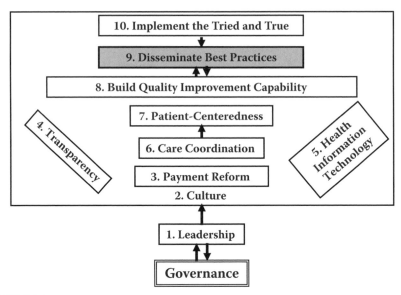

FIGURE 3.1
Top Ten Healthcare Transformers.

In 1601 on a voyage from England to India, Captain James Lancaster tried an experiment by giving 3 teaspoons of lemon juice per person per day on only one of his four ships. Halfway through the journey, 40% of the crew from the three ships who did not get the lemon juice died of scurvy; no crewmembers died of scurvy on the ship that received the lemon juice. Yet, the practice of preventing scurvy was not changed. In 1747, James Lind, a surgeon's mate in the British Royal Navy, also showed that citrus was effective and published *A Treatise of the Scurvy* in 1753. This was termed one of the earliest accounts of a prospective clinical trial, comparing six commonly used treatments of scurvy, but that did not change practice. From 1768 to 1781, Captain James Cook also tested various vegetables and citrus juice as remedies, but dietary practice in the British Navy was not changed. Finally, physician Gilbert Blane in 1795 persuaded the admiral to provide daily rations of lemon juice on all Royal Navy ships. This "mandate" virtually eliminated scurvy overnight in the British Royal Navy, but it was not until 1865 that the British Board of Trade mandated citrus fruit for all merchant marine vessels (Bown 2003). Although a 264-year journey from initial discovery to full implementation may not be the norm, a slow rate of adoption of an innovation is common.

Specific to today's healthcare, the Institute of Medicine (2001) has estimated that it takes up to 17 years to integrate only 30% of clinical recommendations from medical research. Regardless of the specific number, it is the magnitude of the number that is grave to healthcare leaders. The time it takes for important learning to be common practice is substantial, in the form of years. This problem is heightened by the fact that patients' lives and health are at stake.

TRANSFORMER

To effectively disseminate best practices throughout a health system, it is essential to have a dissemination plan in place. As compelling as best practices or improvement results may be, they will not easily transfer to other areas unless a formal plan is designed and monitored to ensure success.

Everett Rogers has published seminal work on the spread of innovations. His writings are foundational to having an effective and efficient dissemination plan. Rogers' biggest contribution is his diffusion of innovations theory (Rogers 1995). Rogers' theory explains that any innovation within a social group is adopted over time by a process he terms natural diffusion (Ransom et al. 2008). Considering the process and the individual characteristics of members of a social group, Rogers categorized adopters along a normal curve as:

- Innovators: 2.5% of the group that are often the first out of the gate; viewed as radicals willing to try a new idea, process, or technology.
- Early adopters: 13.5% of the group that follow the innovators and often include opinion leaders.
- Early majority: 34% of the group that watch the early adopters and begin to form a critical mass for change.
- Late majority: 34% of the group that follow after pressure from peers in the early majority that have embraced the innovation.
- Laggards: 16% of the group that are the last to follow and are resistant to change of an innovation.

When we are spreading change, it is the innovators (2.5% of people) who will be the first to try, followed by the early adopters, early majority, late majority, and then the laggards. A normal bell curve depicts how important it is to find the innovators and early adopters to begin to create the momentum of change for the other groups of people to follow. Trying to convince everyone of the need for change will not achieve the desired result. It is also important to recognize that a person may be an innovator for one topic (like trying a new clinical guideline) but in a different category (such as the late majority) for a different area (like adapting to a new physician referral form). So, it is important to not generalize a laggard or innovator for every innovation but to find the innovators and early adopters for each innovation or improvement in order to get to the mass.

Additionally, Rogers discusses the five stages of adoption of a change:

1. Awareness
2. Interest
3. Evaluation
4. Trial
5. Adoption

Rogers also notes that innovations with certain perceived characteristics will be more likely to move from the first stage of awareness to the final stage of adoption. Rogers states these characteristics as:

- Greater relative advantage (perceived to be better than what is currently done using quantitative and qualitative data)
- Greater compatibility (fits with current needs and values)
- Less complexity (less difficult to perform)
- Great trialability (easy to test)
- Greater observability (easy to see it work)

Considering the work of Rogers and other researchers, IHI has developed a framework (see Figure 3.2) for spread that serves as a useful model for providing a "how-to" approach (Massoud et al. 2006; Nolan et al. 2005). Key elements of this model include:

- Leadership: Ensuring that dissemination is a key strategic activity and that leadership accountability is clear with goals that are aligned with the overall organizational goals.
- Setup: Specifically identifying the target population and the initial strategy to be used for the dissemination—the who, what, and how.
- Better ideas: Considering the important characteristics and evidence so that the new practice is attractive to implement.

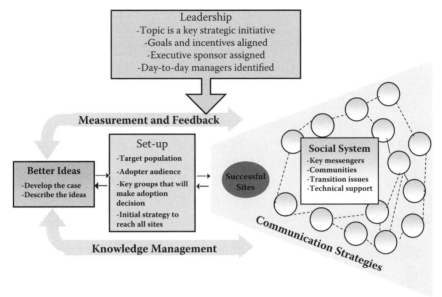

FIGURE 3.2
A framework for spread. (From Massoud, M. R., et al. *A Framework for Spread: From Local Improvements to System-Wide Change.* IHI Innovation Series White Paper. Cambridge, MA: Institute for Healthcare Improvement, 2006. With permission.)

- Communication: Deploying multiple methods to increase awareness and information about the new practices.
- Social system: Understanding the relationships among the people who will be adopting the changes.
- Knowledge management: Managing the knowledge gained as the better practices are spread so that further dissemination is effective.
- Measurement and feedback: Collecting and using data about process and outcomes to better monitor and make adjustments to the dissemination progress.

Many other models exist (Brach et al. 2008). However, regardless of the model or framework used, the most important piece is having a plan in place that is designed up front with clear, measurable goals; is driven by leadership; considers all of the important environmental and social factors that prevent and enable progress; and is monitored and improved for ongoing success.

BEST PRACTICES

An example of how a best practice was spread within a health system is seen in the spread of medication safety practices throughout the ten-hospital Iowa Health System (Iowa Health System 2008). In addition to the use of Leadership WalkRounds, Failure Modes Effects Analysis (FMEA), medication reconciliation, and high-risk drug evaluation, safety unit briefings were one of the primary medication safety practices implemented. Unit briefings, or safety briefings, are brief, daily meetings and conversations with frontline staff to increase awareness of patient safety issues, identify and share important patient safety information, and create a culture of safety.

The Iowa Health System Patient Safety Team developed two specific aims:

1. Spread aim: To spread the use of unit briefings across Iowa Health System's ten hospitals to discover unsafe conditions and opportunities for reducing harm associated with medications. (Unit briefings were one element of the change package for improving medication safety.)
2. Medication safety improvement aim: To reduce adverse drug events tenfold across Iowa Health System in 12 months.

The measures the team used to track the dissemination of the specific changes were:

- Percentage of hospitals using unit briefings, with the goal to spread use of unit briefings to 100% of hospitals and units targeted
- Perspectives of staff participating in the unit briefings
- Percentage of admissions with an adverse drug event across all Iowa Health System hospitals

Iowa Health System first tested the use of unit briefings in one patient unit in one hospital. The unit briefings were then tested in 1 unit at each of 3 pilot hospitals, then spread to 40 units in the first hospital, and subsequently spread across the other health system hospitals in a collaborative process.

Specific changes at the unit level developed through unit briefings included:

- Engaging the pharmacists with nursing units to collaborate on discovering unsafe conditions and ways to improve the processes.
- Improving the knowledge of nurses and pharmacists of best practice activities in medication safety and how these practices apply to the specific units' needs.
- Designing a data collection and feedback mechanism to gather findings and let the units know what happened to their ideas.
- Involving managers in the feedback process.
- Adding implementation of changes discovered through unit briefings to the managers' annual review expectations.

Specific to the improvement of medication safety, the Iowa Health System decreased adverse drug events by 50% in 11 months and a total of 75% in 20 months across the entire health system. Specific to the spread of unit briefings, as shown by Figure 3.3, this best practice was deployed from one unit in one hospital to units throughout the health system in less than 9 months.

The Iowa Health System utilized the IHI spread framework (leadership, set-up, better ideas, communication, social system, knowledge management, and measurement and feedback) as a plan to ensure overall success.

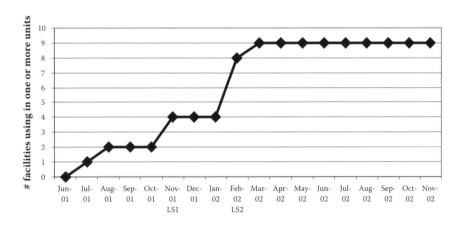

FIGURE 3.3
Iowa Health System: System-wide diffusion—unit briefings.

BOARD QUESTIONS

As a hospital board member, consider these questions:

1. What best practices or improvement initiatives for dissemination should we focus on this year?
2. Is there a plan and mechanism in place to disseminate best practices?
3. What measures are we tracking to ensure effective dissemination of best practices?
4. What do the data show on the spread of our identified improvement efforts?
5. Are we identifying and leveraging early adopters and champions for leading the spread of best practices?
6. What are our biggest barriers to adoption of best practices, and what specific strategies are we using to overcome those barriers?
7. How are our leaders encouraged and incentivized to adopt best practices?
8. What strategies are we using to encourage an environment of dissemination and adoption?

REFERENCES

Berwick, D. M. "Disseminating Innovations in Health Care." *JAMA* 289 (2003): 1969–1975.

Bown, S. R. *Scurvy: How a Surgeon, a Mariner, and a Gentleman Solved the Greatest Medical Mystery of the Age of Sail*. New York: St. Martin's Press, 2003.

Brach, C., N. Lenfestey, A. Roussel, J. Amoozegar, and A. Sorensen. *Will It Work Here? A Decisionmaker's Guide to Adopting Innovations*. AHRQ Publication No. 08-0051. Rockville, MD: Agency for Healthcare Research and Quality, 2008.

Institute of Medicine, Committee on Quality of Health Care in America. *Crossing the Quality Chasm: A New Health System for the 21st Century*. Washington, DC: National Academy Press, 2001.

Iowa Health System. *IHI Improvement Report: Spread of Unit Briefings to Enhance a Culture of Safety*. 2008, http://www.ihi.org/IHI/Topics/Improvement/SpreadingChanges/ImprovementStories/ImprovementReportSpreadofUnitBriefingstoEnhanceACultureofSafety.htm (accessed September 18, 2008).

Massoud, M. R., G. A. Nielsen, K. Nolan, M. W. Schall, and C. Sevin. *A Framework for Spread: From Local Improvements to System-Wide Change*. IHI Innovation Series White Paper. Cambridge, MA: Institute for Healthcare Improvement, 2006.

Nolan, K., M. Schall, F. Erb, and T. Nolan. "Using a Framework for Spread: The Case of Patient Access in the Veterans Health Administration." *Jt Comm J Qual Patient Saf* 31, no. 6 (2005): 339–347.

Ransom E., M. Joshi, D. Nash, and S. Ransom *The Healthcare Quality Book*, 2nd ed. Chicago: Health Administration Press, 2008.

Rogers, E. M. *Diffusion of Innovations*, 4th ed. New York: The Free Press, 1995.

4

Healthcare Transformer 8: Build Organizational Quality Improvement Capability

Healthcare Transformer 8, Build Quality Improvement Capability (see Figure 4.1), is borrowed from other industries in which the capability and competency of an organization to improve is essential. As a transformer in healthcare,

- Organizations must develop frontline and administrative personnel with quality improvement knowledge and skills.

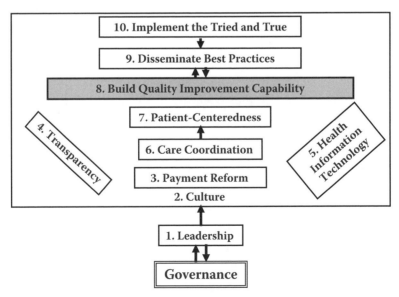

FIGURE 4.1
Top Ten Healthcare Transformers.

- Quality improvement should be taught as a science discipline with specific knowledge and skill areas that are clearly defined by the organization.
- Leadership must require quality improvement capability as necessary for advancement.

This chapter will provide examples of best practices in training and development in quality improvement to better ensure organizational success. The leadership checklist will address the above bullet points of how to develop quality improvement as a science discipline and as an essential leadership trait.

PROBLEM

The building of organizational quality improvement capability is often limited by the following issues:

- Healthcare organizations usually focus on training and education to maintain or improve clinical skills. Far fewer resources, time, and attention are given to training or continuing education programs in quality improvement and patient safety.
- Acquiring quality improvement knowledge is often left to such approaches as memos of patient safety practices, rushed efforts in preparation for an accreditation visit, or sporadic in-services in various departments or units, which may be not well designed, delivered, or attended.
- There is usually a lack of a comprehensive quality improvement training program for the organization. Thus, training may not exist in some departments. If training does exist, the departments may present different quality improvement goals, philosophies, methods, and improvement models with no unifying program.
- Training and education are often not designed strategically to develop a quality improvement capacity but often are limited to specific skills development.

TRANSFORMER

The transformer opportunity to build quality improvement capability includes:

1. Quality improvement vision and approach: It is critical that the organization set forth its quality improvement goals, philosophy, and process improvement model. All three are vital topics for inclusion in any training or development effort.
2. Quality improvement knowledge and skills: The organization must define the key quality improvement knowledge areas and skills desired by the organization.
3. Target groups for development: There are three important groups that should be targeted for quality improvement knowledge and skills: executives/managers, leaders of quality improvement projects, and employees, particularly those who come into contact with patients and other customers.
4. Comprehensive development program: The organization should design an overall program to ensure that it has the experience and knowledge in quality improvement, that training exists for all target groups, and that information is effectively and consistency delivered.
5. Use of all available learning opportunities: The organization should develop additional capability by taking advantage of all learning opportunities, including national conferences and the dissemination of current literature, best practices, and lessons learned from quality improvement projects.
6. Program evaluation and reinforcement: The organization must continually evaluate the effectiveness of its development efforts, continually assess if new knowledge or experience is needed, and provide reinforcement and continuing education as needed.
7. Leadership: Board members and executives must continually emphasize the need for a high level of knowledge and skills in quality improvement and maintain current knowledge in quality improvement.

BEST PRACTICES

The following are key best practices in improving quality improvement capability:

- Leadership: Board members and executives take an active role in quality improvement education by emphasizing the organization's quality improvement goals and philosophy, reviewing training evaluations, and making surprise visits to training sessions.

- Advancement and accountability: Individuals are rewarded and promoted based on their skills and application of quality improvement concepts and approaches, particularly with respect to demonstrated improvement in quality, patient safety, and patient satisfaction indicators.
- Learning through quality conferences and collaboratives: Board members, the senior management team, and key physician leaders attend national conferences and participate in learning collaboratives in quality improvement and patient safety such as those through the Institute of Healthcare Improvement (IHI; http://www.ihi.org).
- Learning through lessons learned: The quality or risk management office documents and distributes lessons learned from morbidity and mortality (M&M) conferences, "near-miss" meetings, and quality improvement projects.
- Learning through literature: The quality office identifies new knowledge from current literature, conferences, and other venues and distributes these to individuals as appropriate.
- Learning through training: The quality office oversees training of the three key target groups in the knowledge and skill areas identified below.

1. All managers (from executives to first-line supervisors)

   ✓ The organization's quality improvement goals, philosophy, and quality/process improvement model
   ✓ Quality improvement theory/concepts
   ✓ Change management
   ✓ Patient safety and risk management concepts and practices
   ✓ Quality/performance indicators
   ✓ The learning organization (innovation, effective use of customer feedback, use of best practices)
   ✓ Leadership practices (continually emphasizing quality and patient safety, creating a no-blame culture, ensuring accountability)
   ✓ Coordinating care

2. Team leaders and facilitators

   ✓ Quality improvement tools (e.g., risk assessment, root-cause analysis, control, and flow charts)
   ✓ Group process/facilitation tools (e.g., brainstorming, nominal group technique, and prioritization techniques)
   ✓ Teambuilding (e.g., goal setting, role clarification, and ground rules for working together)
   ✓ Managing a quality improvement project

3. All employees

   ✓ Service excellence
   ✓ Patient safety practices

- Informal learning: Several less formal, interactive, or reflective opportunities should be explored, including:

  1. Book or journal clubs
  2. Brainstorming sessions on units or in a department on methods to improve quality
  3. Lunch sessions with invited external experts on patient safety
  4. Holding of "chats" on a regular between senior executives and managers to discuss quality issues, exchange approaches to improve care, and share knowledge gained from benchmarking or other outside sources (Scheck McAlearney 2008)

- Comprehensive development program: Catholic Health East (CHE), based in Newtown Square, Pennsylvania, has instituted a comprehensive program that starts with a competency model that outlines the goals and strategies for development at all four management levels: executive, director, managerial, and supervisory. In addition, a "talent management" group (members of the senior team and chief executive officers of system hospitals) reviews the skill sets and training/development activities of all CHE executives (Kaufman and Goldstein 2008).

- Succession planning: Baylor Health System in Dallas uses a multi-rater assessment tool (360 evaluation) to both identify and develop successors for management positions. In addition, Baylor uses a leadership inventory instrument to assess leadership skills to generate self-awareness of areas needing improvement (Kaufman and Goldstein 2008).

BOARD QUESTIONS

As a hospital board member, consider these questions:

1. Do I, as a board member, emphasize the importance of leadership in quality improvement and the need for quality improvement training?
2. Are there formal quality improvement training programs in the organization for (a) all managers, (b) team leaders, and (c) all employees?
3. How are we evaluating the training/development programs? How effective are they in changing attitudes, behaviors, skills, and results?
4. Are there mechanisms in place to track participation in training programs and performance in improving quality, patient safety, and patient satisfaction?
5. Are there succession plans to develop managers for higher levels of responsibility?
6. Is quality improvement a necessary competency for professional advancement and for leadership?

REFERENCES

Kaufman, K., and L. Goldstein. "Leadership and Successful Financial Performance in Healthcare." *Bull Natl Center Healthc Lead* 11 (2008): 9–21.

Scheck McAlearney, A. "Using Leadership Development Programs to Improve Quality and Efficiency in Healthcare. *J Healthc Manage* 53 (2008): 320–331.

5

Healthcare Transformer 7: Patient-Centeredness

There are multiple definitions and models of patient-centeredness, which has also been characterized as person-centered, family-centered, relationship-centered, consumer-focused, and consumer-directed. However, throughout these different descriptions of patient-centeredness, the American Board of Internal Medicine Foundation has identified common themes:

- Respect for patients' preferences, needs, and values.
- Importance of patients' emotional needs and physical and emotional comfort.
- Engagement and dialogue with patients by asking about their needs, listening to their concerns, empathizing, and providing information.
- Incorporation of shared decision-making and promotion of patient autonomy, while also involving family and friends in care decisions when appropriate.
- A more holistic view of healthcare by stressing incorporation of features such as music, art, spiritual issues, and complementary medicine.
- A reflective practitioner who is aware of how his or her emotions and experiences may affect practice.
- Focus on care coordination and continuity over time and within and across care settings (Cunningham 2008).

Irrespective of the nuances of different definitions, patient-centeredness is at the heart of the healthcare profession and for many is the reason that they selected healthcare as their vocation. However, the healthcare system

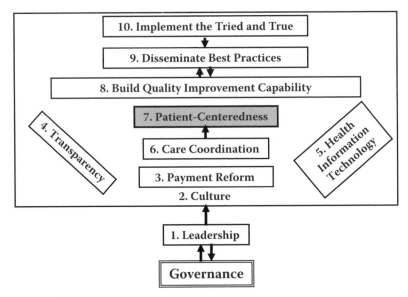

FIGURE 5.1
Top Ten Healthcare Transformers.

is fraught with current systems of care and service in which patient-centeredness is not the driving factor. Compared with the ideal, healthcare falls dramatically short in actual practice of patient-centeredness.

In this chapter, "Healthcare Transformer 7: Patient-Centeredness" (see Figure 5.1), practical and meaningful strategies and tactics in which care can be designed and redesigned for the patient and the family as the center will be discussed.

PROBLEM

Several problems are associated with the lack of patient- and family-centeredness. First, it is critical to have accurate and reliable input from patients and families on their healthcare experiences. With the emergence of the Consumer Assessment of Healthcare Providers and Systems (CAHPS) Hospital Survey, such input is now more valid because it is based on the use of a well-researched survey instrument utilized throughout all hospitals in the country. However, surveys alone do not always provide a complete picture or actionable opportunity of how a hospital's patients and their family members feel about the customer service and medical care they have received. Thus, we still face a major problem for hospitals in receiving and soliciting input from their customers that is useful in taking action.

A related issue is that significant variation exists between hospitals in patients' perceptions of hospital care. Data from 2007 from more than 2,500 hospitals nationwide show that overall 68% of patients would definitely recommend the hospital in which they received care; however, state averages ranged from a low of 58% to a high of 79% (CMS 2008). Individual hospital scores have much greater variation. Additionally, scores of the individual dimensions are also variable and low. The United States average for the quietness of the room and the hospital environment is 56%, communication about medicines is 59%, and responsiveness of hospital staff is 63%. Not only is the variation by hospital substantial, the overall opportunity to improve patient experiences is large.

Building on these two problems, there is a legal and financial impact associated with services that are not patient-centered and result in low patient satisfaction. Numerous studies have shown that the relationship and communication between the patient and the physician, nurse, and staff are significant predictors of complaints, risks, and malpractice claims. The research has shown that:

- The most common cause of malpractice suits is failed communication with patients and their families (Eastaugh 2004; Tongue, Epps, and Forese 2005).
- Patient-centered communication skills are associated with improved health outcomes, increased patient and clinician satisfaction, and less risk of malpractice suits (Fortin 2002).
- A patient-centered approach can facilitate patient disclosure of problems and enhance physician-patient communication, which can improve health outcomes, patient compliance, and patient satisfaction (Barrier, Li, and Jensen 2003).

Patient experience and satisfaction as one defined aspect of patient-centeredness has a dramatic impact on the performance of a hospital in many realms—clinical quality, service, and financial.

Finally, an additional challenge is that the way we provide healthcare today is predominantly not designed to be patient-centered. Thus, to become more patient-centered means fundamentally changing the culture, policies, and practices of hospitals. For example, patient access to medical records is a prevalent issue. Although there are state and federal laws that dictate how patients and families can access their medical records, in practice patients still encounter significant barriers in accessing their own medical records. Culturally, doctors and nurses have been trained to secure medical records and to not make them readily available and open to review. Procedurally, risk management policies have often restricted access to medical records for fear of repercussion and lack of understanding of the information. These issues are not reflective of people's desire, but the system in which practitioners train and work.

Another example is the restriction of visiting hours to hospital intensive care units (ICUs). Although there are many legitimate concerns and barriers to providing more open hours to the ICU for patient visitors, the benefits of a more "liberalized" policy may be profound. Mounting evidence is demonstrating that open ICUs can have a positive impact on reducing patient stress, do not pose an added barrier to clinicians in caring for the patient (and in fact may be supportive to providers), and decrease the anxiety of visitors (Berwick and Kotagal 2004). However, trying or instituting a more liberal visiting hours policy (i.e., being more patient-centered) will require not just a policy change, but a cultural shift on the part of many hospitals. Patient-centeredness necessitates a change in policy, practice, and, most important, philosophy.

TRANSFORMER

Although practically no one would be against patient-centeredness, the reality is that the healthcare industry has not reliably and systematically changed systems so that service and care are focused on patient and family needs. Figure 5.2 displays a roadmap for a six-step plan to assessing, identifying, testing, and evaluating patient-centered approaches.

1. Perform Organizational Self-Assessment → 2. Review Findings →

3. Prioritize Improvement Opportunities → 4. Implement Interventions →

5. Measure and Evaluate Changes → 6. Conduct Periodic Reassessment

FIGURE 5.2
Patient-centeredness implementation roadmap.

1. Perform organizational self-assessment: Through conducting a self-assessment, the organization will better understand its strengths and weaknesses compared with best practices. Examples of tools available to conduct an assessment include the *Patient- and Family-Centered Care Organizational Self-Assessment Tool* from IHI and the National Initiative for Children's Healthcare Quality (2008), the *Planetree and Picker Institute Patient-Centered Guide* (2008), and the Institute for Family-Centered Care Hospital Self-Assessment Inventory (2005). Although the assessment instruments differ in their questions, they generally cover similar major dimensions, such as leadership, mission and values, quality improvement, personnel, information and education, design of the environment, medical charting and documentation, and care support. It is important to obtain multiple perspectives in completing the self-assessment, including those from senior leaders, frontline staff, and patients and families.

2. Review findings: A team should review the self-assessment findings, noting the strengths and weaknesses according to the major dimensions of patient-centeredness.

3. Prioritize improvement opportunities: Using the self-assessment findings, it is critical to prioritize the improvement plans. Resource constraints, largest potential gains, and importance to the mission and strategy of the organization should be considered.

4. Implement interventions: Implementation is where the most problems occur. Implementing interventions requires a disciplined and well-planned improvement project with measurable aims, accountabilities, deadlines, detailed steps, and monitoring. All of these elements are essential to having an improvement project plan with a high yield of success. Emerging interventions that are proving to make significant patient-centered gains include:

   - Involving patients and families on improvement teams
   - Sharing patient stories of medical errors and near misses with leadership and governance
   - Involving patients and families on hospital advisory councils
   - Ensuring that patients and families are part of hospital leadership walkarounds
   - Making patients and families an important part of multidisciplinary daily rounds

- Instituting open and flexible visiting policies on all patient units
- Providing easy access to a patient's health records
- Designing educational materials that are appropriate for the patient population in readability and language
- Offering translation services

5. Measure and evaluate changes: Clear measures and goals for the improvement projects are necessary to make sure projects are achieving intended outcomes or for modifying and testing new interventions if needed.
6. Conduct periodic reassessment: The organization annually completes a self-assessment to provide a milestone progress report.

In summary, the patient-centeredness transformer requires performing an organizational assessment; reviewing the findings; implementing a concrete, measurable plan of improvement; testing interventions that are known to be effective; evaluating the interventions; reassessing; and continuing the cycle again. This continuous improvement process ensures that interventions are purposely planned, implemented, tested, evaluated, and improved.

BEST PRACTICES

Below are three terrific examples of processes and structures that have created more patient-centered healthcare practices.

One example is the impact of an open and flexible visiting policy in the ICU. Results from a pilot, randomized study published in 2006 showed great benefits to having a liberal ICU visitation policy (Fumagalli et al. 2006). In the study, half of the patients decided the number and duration of their visits (an unrestricted visiting policy) compared with the remaining patients who were restricted in their visiting hours (a restricted visiting policy). After appropriate risk adjustment and statistical analyses, the results of the study showed:

- No difference in infections and complications between the two groups.
- Fewer major cardiovascular complications and deaths in the unrestricted visiting policy group.

- Patients in the unrestricted visiting policy group had significantly less anxiety at discharge than admission as well as in comparison to the restricted visiting policy group.

The study's findings suggest the positive clinical impact of a more flexible and open visiting policy in the ICU, which complements the perceived positive social benefits for patients and visitors (Fumagalli et al. 2006).

Another best practice in patient-centeredness is the use of apologies and error disclosure in hospitals. The Veterans Affairs (VA) Medical Center in Lexington, Kentucky, has been operating a formal program in apology and medical error disclosure for more than 20 years. In the program, potentially compensable incidents are identified and reviewed. On the basis of the findings, the hospital provides an open disclosure and discusses compensation options for the family. The hospital accepts responsibility with an apology, the practitioners are involved, and the families are still able to retain an attorney to represent them and pursue another course of action, thus giving them flexibility. In a 13-year period:

- The hospital only went to trial three times.
- The average settlement was $16,000, compared with the national VA averages of a mean malpractice judgment of $413,000, mean settlement pre-trial of $98,000, and mean settlement at trial of $248,165 (Kraman 2008).

Similar impressive outcomes have been reported by a program implemented at the University of Michigan in 2002. As a result of the program, from 2001 to 2005:

- The average time to resolution of claims and lawsuits dropped more than half from 20.7 to 9.5 months.
- The number of claims and lawsuits dropped more than half from 262 to 114.
- The annual litigation costs dropped from $3 million to $1 million (Clinton and Obama 2006).

These few best practices highlight the dramatic impact on financial and patient outcomes that the implementation of patient-centered programs can have as culture changes and new practices are put in place.

BOARD QUESTIONS

As a hospital board member, consider these questions:

1. How do we collect patient and family experience information for our planning and improvement?
2. How valid is our patient input?
3. Have we used one of the commonly available toolkits to perform an organizational assessment regarding patient-centeredness?
4. What are our biggest gaps and improvement opportunities in patient-centeredness?
5. How are we progressing toward patient-centeredness goals?
6. How are patients and families involved in the design of our improvement efforts?
7. How are patients and families engaged in their care?
8. Are we taking a more holistic view of healthcare by considering incorporation of features such as music, art, spiritual issues, and complementary medicine?
9. Are there evidenced-based patient-centered interventions that we should try implementing; for example, sharing patient stories of medical errors and near misses at board meetings, testing apologies, disclosures of errors, including patients on improvement teams, creating patient and family advisory councils, and making medical records more accessible to patients?
10. Are we measuring our organization's culture toward being more patient-centered?

REFERENCES

Barrier, P.A., J. T. Li, and N. M. Jensen. "Two Words to Improve Physician-Patient Communication: What Else?" *Mayo Clin Proc* 78, no. 2 (2003): 211–214.

Berwick, D. M., and M. Kotagal. "Restricted Visiting Hours in ICUs: Time to Change." *JAMA* 292, no. 6 (2004): 736–737.

Centers for Medicare and Medicaid Services (CMS). *Summary of HCAHPS Survey Results.* Baltimore: CMS, 2008, http://www.hcahpsonline.org (accessed October 25, 2008).

Clinton, H. R., and B. Obama. "Making Patient Safety the Centerpiece of Medical Liability Reform." *N Engl J Med* 354, no. 21 (2006): 2205–2208.

Cunningham, A. *Synthesis of Definitions of Patient-, Family- and Relationship-Centered Care.* Presented at the ABIM Foundation 2008 Forum, July 26–29, 2008, in Yountville Napa Valley, CA.

Eastaugh, S. R. "Reducing Litigation Costs through Better Patient Communication." *Physician Exec* 30, no. 3 (2004): 36–38.

Fortin, A. H. "Communication Skills to Improve Patient Satisfaction and Quality of Care." *Ethn Dis* 12, no. 4, Suppl. 3 (2002): 58–61.

Fumagalli, S., L. Boncinelli, A. Lo Nostro, P. Valoti, G. Baldereschi, M. Di Bari, A. Ungar, et al. "Reduced Cardiocirculatory Complications with Unrestrictive Visiting Policy in an Intensive Care Unit: Results from a Pilot, Randomized Trial." *Circulation* 113, no. 7 (2006): 946–952.

Institute for Family-Centered Care. *Strategies for Leadership. Patient- and Family-Centered Care: A Hospital Self-Assessment Inventory.* 2005, http://www.aha.org/aha/content/2005/pdf/assessment.pdf (accessed October 25, 2008).

Institute for Healthcare Improvement (IHI) and National Initiative for Children's Healthcare Quality. *Patient- and Family-Centered Care Organizational Self-Assessment Tool.* 2008, http://www.ihi.org/IHI/Topics/PatientCenteredCare/PatientCenteredCareGeneral/EmergingContent/PFCCOrgSelfAssess.htm (accessed October 25, 2008).

Kraman, S. *Victim Compensation without Litigation: The Lexington Experience.* 2008, http://www.sorryworks.net/files/Kraman-Presentation.ppt (accessed October 25, 2008).

Planetree. *Planetree and Picker Institute Patient-Centered Guide.* 2008, http://www.planetree.org/Events/pcam.html (accessed October 25, 2008).

Tongue, J. R., H. R. Epps, and L. L. Forese. "Communication Skills." *Instr Course Lect* 54 (2005): 3–9.

6

Healthcare Transformer 6: Care Coordination

Transformer 6, care coordination (see Figure 6.1), is an emerging challenge in our healthcare system because of the increasing complexity of the number of providers, number of settings of care, and the number of methods of delivering care. Coordinating care across services within your hospital (such as between diagnostic imaging and a patient unit), across settings (such as between the intensive care unit and the medicine floor), or across people (such as between a primary doctor and specialist) is a challenge no matter who or where you are. Although we talk about "seam-

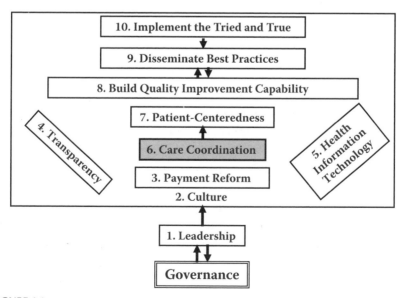

FIGURE 6.1

Top Ten Healthcare Transformers.

less care," the healthcare industry has failed miserably in achieving it and it is often recognized as a main driver for poor quality and medical error.

This chapter will use specific examples of coordination of care—handoffs and transitions in the hospital—to highlight care coordination issues. There are several interventions that hospitals are implementing today to address gaps in care coordination, including better systems of communication, personnel resourcing, and information technology. Healthcare continues to change in terms of where care is delivered and by whom; thus, care coordination becomes more vulnerable as a cause of poor care and service.

PROBLEM

The importance of improving coordination of care and communication among healthcare providers and settings can be seen in the following issues:

- Agency for Healthcare Research and Quality (AHRQ) (2008b) reported that poor coordination of care more than quadruples the odds of medical error.
- A recent report to Congress documented that 17.6% of Medicare patients were readmitted to the hospital within 30 days (Commonwealth Fund 2008).
- A study at Massachusetts General Hospital found that 59% of residents stated that one or more patients had been harmed during their most recent clinical rotation because of problematic handoffs, and that 12% reported that this harm had been major (Kitch et al. 2008).
- A study of malpractice claims in an emergency department showed that approximately 25% of missed diagnoses were caused by an inadequate handoff (e.g., failure to get a positive lab result back to the ordering physician) (Kachalia et al. 2007).
- Parchman, Hitchcock, and Shuko (2005) found that 45% of patients with a chronic illness reported they received no help from their doctor or health plan in coordinating their medical services.
- Dayton and Henriksen (2007) identified in their literature review that poor communication was:

1. The largest contributor to wrong site surgery and delays in treatment
2. The second most common cause for medication errors, patient falls, and adverse events during and after an operation
3. Responsible for 91% of mishaps involving medical residents

• The results of an AHRQ hospital culture survey showed that hospital staff's perception about handoffs and transitions was positive at only 45%. For the following four questions, staff indicated a very poor rating:

1. Things fall between the cracks when transferring patients from one unit to another.
2. Important patient care information is often lost during shift changes.
3. Problems often occur in the exchange of information across hospital units.
4. Shift changes are problematic for patients in this hospital (AHRQ 2008a).

TRANSFORMER

The transformer opportunity includes:

1. Care coordinators/linking pins: These could be physicians (e.g., hospitalists), nurses or social workers (case managers), or administrative staff who coordinate referrals, follow up on test results, and ensure effective information transfers among settings or providers.
2. Interdisciplinary coordination: This includes joint rounding of patients, establishing procedures for coordination, and teambuilding.
3. Structured communication: This includes read-backs of orders and instructions, briefings before a medical procedure, and a structured communication tool or checklist when handing off a patient to another provider.
4. Tracking and follow-up systems: This includes computer systems and programs that identify the treatment needs (protocol or plan)

for a patient, track the patient's progress, and send reminders for needed follow-up (exams, tests, and procedures).

BEST PRACTICES

The practices in common with organizations that have successfully improved care coordination are:

- Teambuilding: This usually consists of clarifying roles, establishing working relationships and interpersonal communication among providers, and setting ground rules for teamwork (e.g., question and participate, listen constructively, seek clarification and understanding, and speak up when in doubt or if concerned about a patient).
- Crew resource management training: Borrowed from the aviation industry and successfully applied in healthcare, this is interactive training and teambuilding for the healthcare team in such areas as structured communication approaches, assertiveness, and ground rules for teamwork and collaboration.
- Interdisciplinary problem-solving meetings: These are regular meetings of physicians, nurses, therapists, social workers, and pharmacists to discuss coordination, quality, service, and other issues in a patient care unit.
- SBAR (Situation, Background, Assessment, Recommendation): This is a structured communication method to relay critical patient information or concerns about a patient. For example, a nurse would describe to a physician, the "situation" (e.g., trouble with breathing), the "background" (e.g., 60-year-old with chronic lung disease), his/her "assessment" (e.g., "I think he has a pneumothorax"), and "recommendation" (e.g., "I think you should come in right now because I think he needs a chest tube") (Bisognano and Lloyd 2007).
- "Touch base" meeting: This is a brief, daily meeting between a physician and nursing team leader or manager on the status of each patient before the physician leaves the unit.
- Joint rounding: This ensures all clearly know the current status and treatment plan for the patients. Rounds should include all those

providing care to the patient, including nurses, therapists, and house staff (residents, interns) if applicable.

- The OR brief (an expanded "time out"): This is a meeting immediately before an operation commences. Here critical information is verified (e.g., correct patient, site, procedure, and administration of antibiotics) and potential risks (e.g., bleeding and fluid loss) and contingency plans are identified.

- Patient information systems: As mentioned earlier these are computer programs that use algorithms or protocols that lay out treatment needs; track the patient's progress; and send reminders for follow-up exams, tests, and procedures.

- Leadership: Most critical is the role of the leader who must ensure that coordinating mechanisms are in place. In addition, leaders/managers at all levels must emphasize ongoing and one-on-one communication and coordination (e.g., "just pick up the phone and call").

- Case management and discharge planning: Many organizations use a case manager (usually a nurse or social worker) to arrange and follow up on referrals and other patient care needs among providers. In addition, interdisciplinary discharge planning meetings are held to ensure follow-up care and social services, if needed, are provided after discharge.

- Patient liaison: Some healthcare organizations use an administrative staff member or social worker to assist the patient and family in navigating the health system, particularly for patients with complex or chronic conditions. In addition, many organizations establish a formal relationship with a family member (e.g., son of an elderly patient) to ensure follow-up of referrals, procedures, etc.

- Linking pins: These are hospital representatives who meet on a regular basis with office managers and providers who refer patients to the hospital. Critical to the discussions are the efficacy and timeliness of reports, patient information, and follow-up care.

- Clinical/nurse advocates: Catholic Health Partners, based in Cincinnati, Ohio, has trained and uses nurses called "heart failure advocates" to educate patients about their disease, coordinate their care, and follow up with them after discharge. These advocates go beyond the roles of the case managers, discharge planners, patient liaisons, and linking pins described previously. They have been charged to do "whatever it takes" to improve heart failure (HF) care and the patient's quality of life. They look for way to improve systems of care, use evidence-based clinical guidelines, continually coordinate between outpatient providers and the patient, educate and follow up with patients on their diets, implement behavioral strategies to increase medication adherence, and address post-discharge barriers. For example, they assist low-income patients with obtaining medications through pharmaceutical company programs that offer free or low-cost prescription drugs. The results across the 22 Catholic Partner Hospitals have been astounding. There was a 40% decline in inpatient HF mortality rates, and HF patients were 5 times less likely to be readmitted within 30 days (Commonwealth Fund 2008).

- Handoff system: Great Ormond Street Hospital (GOSH) in London, England, used Ferrari Formula One pit crew team consultants to design a better system for handoffs between the operating room (OR) and the intensive care unit (ICU). GOSH learned that one of the important roles in pit crew coordination was that of the "Lollipop Man"—the member of the crew who holds up a large round sign that resembles a lollipop and signals to the driver when to stop and leave. Hence, the Lollipop Man highlights the need for timely, accurate information and sequencing of activities. Like healthcare, this informational role is critical because crewmembers could be run over if coordination and information fails. The following were key redesign features to improve the OR-ICU handoff:

1. Training each hospital staff member for a specific task set
2. Developing protocols for each member of the team
3. Having a "carer" (designated person) to ensure adequate information, equipment, supplies, and other support services
4. Sequencing of the steps
5. Using a "Lollipop Man" (an anesthesiologist) to monitor the sequence and to provide clear signals to every member of the care team

The results were extremely positive. Errors per handoff to the ICU fell by 42% and the number of information omissions fell by 49% (Bisognano and Conway 2008).

BOARD QUESTIONS

As a hospital board member, consider these questions:

1. What measures are we using to track care coordination within the hospital and with other providers and stakeholders in the community and how are we doing?
2. Do I, as a board member, emphasize the importance of communication among providers within my organization and with referral providers and other entities that we interact with to ensure effective coordination and continuity of care?
3. Specifically, how do we ensure effective transitions and handoffs of information and care across shifts within the hospital?
4. Are there effective mechanisms in place for coordination within my organization such as joint rounding, OR briefings, case management, and discharge planning?
5. Are there effective mechanisms (e.g., use of patient liaisons) in place to assist patients in navigating the healthcare systems?
6. Am I advancing information management systems, particularly electronic health records, which would track and follow up on patient care needs?
7. Are we tracking our hospital's readmission rates?
8. Have we examined the main causes of avoidable readmissions and identified opportunities for improvement?
9. For factors that are outside of the hospital's control, are we working with community stakeholders to reduce avoidable readmissions?

REFERENCES

Agency for Healthcare Research and Quality (AHRQ). *Hospital Survey on Patient Safety Culture: 2008 Comparative Database Report.* AHRQ Publication No. 08-0039. Rockville, MD: AHRQ, 2008a, http://www.ahrq.gov/qual/hospsurvey08/ (accessed September 22, 2008).

Agency for Healthcare Research and Quality (AHRQ). *Patient Safety and Quality: Patient Complaints about Poor Coordination of Care or Other Services May Help Identify Patient Safety Hazards.* 2008b, http://www.ahrq.gov/research/jul08/0708RA6.htm (accessed November 18, 2008).

Bisognano, M., and J. Conway. *10 Powerful Ideas for Improving Patient Care: Book 4.* Chicago: Health Administration Press, 2008.

Bisognano, M. and R. Lloyd. *10 Powerful Ideas for Improving Patient Care: Book 3*. Chicago: Health Administration Press, 2007.

Commonwealth Fund. "Hospital Readmissions." *Quality Matters*, 2008, http://www.commonwealthfund.org/publications/publications_show.htm?doc_id=673140 (accessed November 17, 2008).

Dayton E., and K. Henriksen. "Communication Failure: Basic Components, Contributing Factors, and the Call for Structure." *Jt Comm J Qual Patient Saf* 33 (2007): 34–47.

Kachalia, A., T. K. Gandhi, A. L. Puopolo, C. Yoon, E. J. Thomas, R. Griffey, T. A. Brennan, and D. M. Studdert. "Missed and Delayed Diagnosis in the Emergency Department: A Study of Closed Malpractice Claims from 4 Liability Insurers." *Ann Emerg Med* 49 (2007): 196–205.

Kitch, B. T., J. B. Cooper, W. M. Zapol, J. E. Marder, A. Karson, M. Hutter, and E.G. Campbell. "Handoffs Causing Patient Harm: A Survey of Medical and Surgical House Staff." *Jt Comm J Qual Patient Saf* 34 (2008): 563–570.

Parchman, M. L., N. P. Hitchcock, and L. Shuko. "Primary Care Attributes, Health Care System Hassles, and Chronic Illness." *Med Care* 43 (2005): 1123–1129.

7

Healthcare Transformer 5: Health Information Technology

Technology advancement has served as the foundation of disruptive innovations in many industries. Leveraging the widespread use of the Internet, organizations such as eBay, Yahoo, MapQuest, MySpace, and Google have all utilized technology to create new markets, new customers, new revenue sources, and new businesses.

The promise of the impact of health information technology (HIT) on better health and healthcare is profound. Although there are many HIT systems (e.g., picture archiving and communication systems, laboratory ordering and results tracking, clinical data repository, dictation, master patient indexing, operating room scheduling, electronic prescribing, and barcode medication administration), three HIT programs that will play a substantial role in healthcare transformation are:

- Computerized prescriber order entry (CPOE)
- Electronic health records (EHRs)
- Personalized health records (PHRs)

Healthcare Transformer 5 (Figure 7.1) focuses on the optimal implementation of HIT to achieve better healthcare outcomes and make our health system more efficient.

PROBLEM

The use of paper, manual processes, and the lack of clinical decision support systems have been key reasons for medical errors and patient and

FIGURE 7.1
Top Ten Healthcare Transformers.

provider dissatisfaction. Medication errors are very common, as shown by the following estimates:

- Over 1 million serious medication errors occur in U.S. hospitals every year (Kuperman et al. 2007).
- Twenty percent of errors are life-threatening adverse drug events (Kelly and Rucker 2006; Van der Sijs et al. 2006).
- Medication errors cost our country $2 billion in hospital costs alone (Birkmeyer and Dimick 2004).

There are a multitude of medication error categories, including giving the wrong dose, the wrong drug, wrong administration of the drug, a drug-drug interaction, or a drug-allergy interaction. These errors occur for numerous reasons, including poor or illegible handwriting, lack of awareness or knowledge of the patient's medicine list and allergies, and lack of awareness and knowledge of general drug information and interactions.

The antiquated paper-based medical record system in healthcare is also a primary cause for delays in treatment, waste of time between the provider and patient, and increased medical mistakes. Consider the following:

- Paper medical records need to physically move from doctor to doctor and hospital unit to hospital unit, all contributing to a greater chance of missing or lost information.

- Time is wasted with staff searching for paper medical records.
- Access to paper records is very insecure.
- Writing the decimal place in the wrong spot of a prescription amount on paper can lead to drug overdose and death (Centers for Disease Control and Prevention 2007).
- A paper-based medical information system makes it difficult to reliably generate reminders for patients for treatment services and follow-up tests.

Our healthcare system is filled with paper, which causes great inefficiency in time and resources and has led to a tremendous level of medical errors and worse healthcare. A paper-based system means more dependence on human processes and memory, which are less reliable and lead to more mistakes.

TRANSFORMER

The implementation of HIT has a major, positive impact on all key players in the healthcare system. Although there is no perfect system, the presence of a system can help providers deliver better care and help patients and families be more involved in the management of their own care.

CPOE systems play a crucial role in reducing medication errors in the hospital. CPOE systems replace paper prescription forms by allowing prescribers (most often physicians) to electronically submit drug prescriptions. With the computer system, prescriptions are electronically transmitted to the pharmacy, and the system will detect orders that may interact adversely with other drugs the patient is taking and dosages that are outside of the normal ranges. Through electronic submission, CPOE systems play an important role in decreasing the delay of prescriptions, reducing errors from handwriting mistakes and incorrect transcription, and preventing errors in the wrong and duplicate dosage of medicines. The evidence shows that CPOE systems can reduce medication errors by 80%, and although the cost is high, it is estimated that the savings can pay for the hospital's investment in 26 months (Koppel et al. 2005; Massachusetts Technology Collaborative and New England Healthcare Institute 2008).

EHRs, first known as electronic medical records (EMRs), are simply the electronic conversion of the paper medical chart into a digital medium.

EHRs include a patient's medical history, test results, current medicines, treatment plans, and information that can help the doctor manage the patient's health. In a simple analogy, EHRs may be compared to computer accounting systems. Errors can more readily happen in paper general ledgers and the use of the general ledger information in producing and tracking financial information. These errors may be writing down the wrong dollar amounts, transposing information, and using the information to produce incorrect income statements. Software accounting systems ensure that numbers reconcile and automatically produce statements based on entered information. EHRs play a similar role in aiding the correct entry and use of clinical information to manage a patient's health. Because EHRs are early in their implementation, the evidence on their impact is emerging. However, anecdotally, EHRs have demonstrated improved quality of patient care, enhanced efficiency in documentation, and reduced costs through better management of test ordering and treatment plans (NIH National Center for Research Resources 2006).

PHRs are a complement to EHRs as records for use by patients. PHRs allow patients to view, enter, and track their own medical information, such as history, medicines, and test results, and can facilitate communication with the doctor. PHRs come in multiple forms, such as Web-based systems or electronic files stored on a Universal Serial Bus (USB) flash drive. PHRs allow the patient to utilize simple, easy-to-access electronic media rather than handling multiple pieces of paper. Similar to EHRs, PHRs are in their infancy of adoption. The perceived benefits of PHRs are significant, including:

- Greater engagement of patients in their medical condition and treatment
- Better care as a result of increased awareness of their health information and treatment plan
- More accurate health information, which can reduce unnecessary tests

The HIT transformer requires a hospital to:

- Conduct an assessment to identify the gaps for implementation
- Develop a detailed roadmap
- Learn from other sites that have experience and expertise with implementation
- Identify champions and areas with which to start

- Provide ongoing education and support
- Go beyond technology and pay attention to change management, work flow redesign, human resource implications, and leadership drive
- Stay focused on implementation

HIT systems are not ideal today. If not well planned and implemented, such systems may not achieve their full benefits. However, healthcare must embrace technology to further health outcomes. Technology will continue to develop rapidly, and hospitals must continue to work on the effective and efficient implementation of HIT to achieve their maximum potential.

BEST PRACTICES

More and more case studies are demonstrating the value of HIT for improved cost and quality of patient care. Because HIT is early in its implementation cycle, the published literature is small but growing, with CPOE systems possessing the largest body of work and demonstrating its positive impact on many health systems.

One example is that of Baptist Health Systems in Jackson, Mississippi. Baptist utilized multiple HIT systems, including barcode medication administration and CPOE. Starting with the strategic focus on patient safety and quality, the organization conducted a medication management review with McKesson , a company that specializes in information technology, to identify risk areas and appropriate HIT solutions. After selecting a vendor and system using a team approach, the hospital invested heavily in engagement of staff with visible leadership leverage. Overall, the results are profound and in line with other hospital success stories. With CPOE and other supplementary medication systems, the hospital observed:

- A decrease of 38% in the time from order to delivery of drugs
- A reduction of 2,000 pharmacy hours (1 FTE) annually through less wasted time and improved productivity
- Increased nursing productivity
- Cost savings (McKesson 2008)

Another example is the implementation of HIT at the University of Illinois Medical Center (UIMC), the largest state-funded hospital

(Ranganathan and Watson-Manheim 2004). Over a 6-year effort, UIMC implemented a vast array of applications, with the core being an electronic patient record (EPR). With EPR in the center, the entire system contains medical data on more than 2 million patients (including patient demographics, insurance, medical histories, medication charting, nursing and physician notes, and lab reports) available from multiple access points, including remote access via the Internet. Caregivers can remotely order diagnostic tests and view results within minutes of their availability. The system also features decision support and knowledge management components, which alert clinicians to potential adverse drug events and reactions. The benefits and value are powerful.

- Before the system's implementation, patient health records were unavailable approximately 40% of the time. After implementation, records are accessible 100% of the time.
- More than 5,000 annual radiologist hours have been saved, and approximately $1.2 million of nurses' time reallocated to patient care.
- Average time to receive laboratory and test results has dropped from 3 days to just seconds after availability.
- The stack of paper associated with each patient has decreased from approximately 300 pages to less than 75 and this continues to drop every year.

What should not be lost in the written succinctness of these two examples and their results is the significant planning and leadership commitment it took to put these HIT solutions in place and achieve the results in improved productivity, reduced costs, and improved quality. Without the purposeful design, patience, and backing from leadership and governance, these results would have been much more difficult and time consuming to accomplish.

BOARD QUESTIONS

As a hospital board member, consider these questions:

1. What is our HIT strategic and operating plan?
2. Are we on track with the implementation of our various HIT systems?

3. What is our status in HIT implementation, specifically of CPOE systems, EHRs, and PHRs?
4. Is our HIT plan connecting partners in our community, that is, with other doctors, other healthcare providers, and other settings of care?
5. How are we encouraging greater use of PHRs?
6. Are we tracking and have we improved patient health outcomes and other key indicators as a result of HIT?
7. Are we measuring the cost-effectiveness of our HIT systems?
8. Are we constantly asking ourselves how we can leverage HIT to improve quality and safety?

REFERENCES

Birkmeyer, J. D., and J. B. Dimick. *Leapfrog Safety Standards: Potential Benefits of Universal Adoption.* Washington, DC: The Leapfrog Group, 2004.

Centers for Disease Control and Prevention. "Unintentional Poisoning Deaths—United States, 1999–2004." *MMWR Morb Mortal Wkly Rep* 56, no. 5 (2007): 93–96.

Kelly, W. N., and T. D. Rucker. "Compelling Features of a Safe Medication-Use System." *Am J Health Syst Pharm* 63, no. 15 (2006): 1461–1468.

Koppel, R., J. P. Metlay, A. Cohen, B. Abaluck, A. R. Localio, S. E. Kimmel, and B. L. Strom. "Role of Computerized Physician Order Entry Systems in Facilitating Medication Errors." *JAMA* 293, no. 10 (2005): 1197–1203.

Kuperman, G. J., A. Bobb, T. H. Payne, A. J. Avery, T. K. Gandhi, G. Burns, D. C. Classen, et al. "Medication-Related Clinical Decision Support in Computerized Provider Order Entry Systems: A Review." *J Am Med Inform Assoc* 14, no. 1 (2007): 29–40.

Massachusetts Technology Collaborative and New England Healthcare Institute. *Saving Lives, Saving Money: The Imperative for CPOE in Massachusetts.* 2008, http://web3. streamhoster.com/mtc/cpoe20808.pdf (accessed November 1, 2008).

McKesson. *Case Study: Baptist Health Systems.* 2008, http://www.mckesson.com/static_ files/McKesson.com/MPT/Documents/VIP2008_BaptistHealthSystems_PRT340. pdf (accessed November 2, 2008).

National Institutes of Health (NIH) National Center for Research Resources. *Electronic Health Records Review.* 2006, http://www.ncrr.nih.gov/publications/informatics/ EHR.pdf (accessed November 1, 2008).

Ranganathan, C., and M. Watson-Manheim. *Curing Hospitals' Ills.* IBM, 2004.

Van der Sijs, H., J. Aarts, A. Vulto, and M. Berg. "Overriding of Drug Safety Alerts in Computerized Physician Order Entry." *J Am Med Inform Assoc* 13, no. 2 (2006): 138–147.

8

Healthcare Transformer 4: Transparency

More public reporting of quality information is a major trend today in healthcare. How is your hospital responding?

Transparency has been, and will continue to be, a transformative factor in our healthcare system (see Figure 8.1). This chapter will provide examples of public reporting that have spurred organizations to increased quality improvement efforts and examine how consumers, to a much lesser extent, are using data for decision-making and discussion with their providers.

The leadership message from this transformer is to embrace transparency as a change agent—whether it is to provide public reporting of your

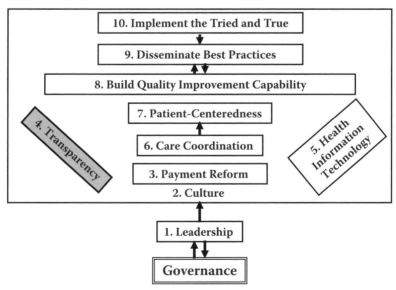

FIGURE 8.1
Top Ten Healthcare Transformers.

organization's quality outcomes, employee and patient satisfaction survey results, ethics policies, or conflicts of interest.

PROBLEM

Without transparency, it is difficult to make informed decisions. For example, one only needs to look to the recent global subprime mortgage crisis to see the risks associated with inadequate public reporting of financial information. Buyers of mortgage-backed securities and collateralized debt obligations did not fully realize the risky nature of their investments. Trust was placed in the high credit ratings such investments received because sufficient information was not available about the nature of the individual assets and how the credit ratings were assigned (Kroszner 2008). Greater transparency is needed to "give all parties better tools to monitor financial risk-taking themselves" (Baily and Litan 2008).

Without readily accessible quality information, consumers are similarly hampered in their healthcare choices. A 2006 study found that 95% of adults want information on the quality of care provided by doctors and hospitals; 91% want to know the costs of care prior to care delivery (Schoen et al. 2006). However, a 2004 survey found that only 35% of Americans had encountered information comparing quality among health insurance plans, hospitals, and/or doctors in the previous year, and only 19% used such information in making healthcare decisions (KFF, AHRQ, and Harvard School of Public Health 2004). These results reflect a slight improvement from the previous survey conducted in 2000 in which 27% of Americans reported seeing quality information and just 12% used such information for healthcare decisions (KFF et al. 2004). Top reasons for not using quality information included not needing to make relevant healthcare decisions at that time, lack of information specificity to personal health conditions or concerns, and placing greater importance on other factors, including location or cost (KFF et al. 2004).

Although consumer use of healthcare quality information is still growing, there is evidence that public reporting has increased quality improvement efforts by healthcare providers. Schneider and Lieberman (2001, 101) note that "outcomes and performance appear to be improving in some areas. If public disclosure of report cards has an effect, it is because disclosure focuses health plans, hospitals, and other providers to address issues of healthcare quality that may in the past have been ignored."

For example, Hibbard, Stockard, and Tusler (2003) found that Wisconsin hospitals with publicly reported performance information (public report hospitals) had more quality improvement efforts compared with hospitals that only received private reports on performance (private report hospitals) and hospitals that received no performance reports (no report hospitals). The pattern that public report hospitals engaged in more quality improvement activities than private report hospitals, which engaged in more improvement activities than no report hospitals, was evident in obstetric care and cardiac care outcomes reporting.

"Public disclosure appears to galvanize providers into action, either because they perceive a threat to their reputations or because it is an opportunity to market their excellence" (Schneider and Lieberman 2001, 101). This may explain the substantial improvement in hospital quality-of-care data for acute myocardial infarction, congestive heart failure, and pneumonia seen in the Hospital Quality Alliance (HQA) program in just 18 months. "The improvement was even more dramatic in the treatment of pneumonia and heart failure, for which performance had been low in the first analysis. The data also showed that, for all three conditions, the gap between the scores of the worst-performing hospitals and the best-performing hospitals narrowed" (Klein 2007, 2).

In addition to public reporting of quality information, internal transparency or open book management has been shown to improve employee satisfaction, reduce turnover, and improve performance. Open book management relies on "sound measurement and analysis of clinical, operational, and financial data, as well as clear, broadly disseminated communication of that information" (Gelinas and Loh 2004). In examining the cultural best practices of VHA hospitals that have received formal Employer of Choice recognition, Gelinas and Loh (2004) found that leadership development, performance management, and open book management appeared to have the greatest overall effect on performance. Data for the hospitals showed that "they not only had a lower 3-year average turnover rate in full-time staff compared to the worst performing hospitals, but that this difference also represented by more than $3.5 million in lower replacement costs" (Gelinas and Loh 2004). Previous research from VHA hospitals showed that organizations with lower turnover rates had lower risk-adjusted mortality scores and average length of stay (Gelinas and Loh 2004).

TRANSFORMER

As a hospital board member, you can use public reporting as a tool to assess the organization's performance and areas for improvement. Leaders often worry about public perception of hospital performance once data are publicly reported. However, do not let perfect be the enemy of very good. Be transparent with your own data internally and externally. Use your hospital website to share quality information, employee and patient satisfaction survey data, ethics policies, and conflicts of interest. Clearly communicate that your hospital is dedicated to improving the community's health, and to do so, you must enhance our own systems.

It may be helpful to think of the transformative opportunity to increase transparency in terms of the following model, which incorporates four key factors:

1. Establish clear transparency values: Develop sound transparency principles to guide decisions. Essential questions to ask include
   - What organizations are we comparing ourselves to?
   - What are our goals?
   - What measures do we use?
   - What information do we share?
   - Are we reporting positive and negative data?
2. Draw meaningful comparisons: Set appropriate goals to ensure significant comparisons.
   - Compare your performance over time to track progress.
   - Compare your performance to others—not just the state or national average, but a benchmark. For example, compare short- and long-term goals with the best in your own health system, to the best in the state, to the best in the nation, and to the best among your peers. Avoid complacency with your comparisons. Remember that benchmarks can serve as a floor or a ceiling.
3. Create accountability for results: Build accountability by reviewing measures and linking them to financial performance. Translate data into lives saved, complications avoided, and dollars saved. Use metrics that make the gaps more understandable and meaningful in terms of individuals affected. For example, 90% might seem good, but not when 10% could mean an infection a day. Tie increased transparency to employee incentives as appropriate.

4. Acknowledge the journey: Much progress is yet to come in the area of transparency. We need to improve in measuring and using data, publicizing the availability of quality data, and helping consumers to understand the information.

Partner with the community to improve. Explain the quality goals that your hospital is working toward, how you plan to meet those goals, and the timetable for your efforts.

BEST PRACTICES

Norton Healthcare, Kentucky's largest not-for-profit health system, exemplifies today's best practices in healthcare quality information transparency. Norton voluntarily publishes patient satisfaction scores and performance for its hospitals on almost 600 quality indicators and practices (Norton Healthcare 2008). The organization's quality report is available online and updated monthly or more frequently as data become available. Norton reports on nationally recognized indicators from the National Quality Forum, the Agency for Healthcare Research and Quality, the Joint Commission on Accreditation of Healthcare Organizations, the Centers for Medicare & Medicaid Services, the Vermont Oxford Network, Press Ganey Associates, and the National Cancer Database. Below are Norton's quality report principles:

- We do not decide what to make public on the basis of how it makes us look.
- We give equal prominence to good and bad results.
- We do not choose which indicators to display.
- When we have a nationally endorsed list of indicators, we display every indicator on the list.
- We are not the indicator owner.
- We do not modify indicator definitions or inclusion/exclusion criteria in any way.
- We only correct our internal data for objective errors.
- We do not correct data submitted or billed externally unless we also re-submit or re-bill the data. We display results even when we disagree with the indicator definition.

- We believe unused data never become valid.
- We recognize that we must display and make decisions based upon imperfect data, because until the data are used, no resources will be spent making the data valid (Norton Healthcare 2008).

The health system notes that "public reporting has helped us document our care more carefully, obtain more valid data, and give better patient care than we would have without public reporting" (Norton Healthcare 2008). Although we have no formal evidence that public reporting has affected Norton Healthcare's overall performance and bottom line, the organization's financial performance has continued to improve since introducing the quality report in 2005.

Another outstanding example of transparency is INTEGRIS Health, Oklahoma's largest not-for-profit healthcare organization. INTEGRIS provides quality, price, and customer satisfaction information on its website for the hospitals in its system. The organization aims to be "both accountable and transparent to our patients and the public" (INTEGRIS Health 2008).

INTEGRIS clearly explains the types of measures it uses to evaluate quality—structure, process, and outcome—as well as its quality goals: "We consider we are doing reasonably well if our numbers are 95% or better, but our ultimate goal is to do things right, 100% of the time" (INTEGRIS Health 2008). For each quality measure, INTEGRIS shows—in tabular and graphic formats—individual hospital performance data in comparison to the statewide and national averages as well as to the top 10% of U.S. hospitals.

For patient satisfaction information, INTEGRIS provides inpatient, outpatient, and emergency department data in comparison to national averages. Patient comments and changes made in response to survey comments are also listed. Regarding price data, INTEGRIS offers an interactive bill sample on its website, with an explanation of each bill section. Patients wanting prices for specific procedures may either submit an online request or call a toll-free number, with pricing information available 24 hours a day, 7 days a week. Patients are promised an estimate within 2 business days. Figure 8.2 is a screen shot of INTEGRIS Health's web section on Quality, Pricing, and Patient Satisfaction (INTEGRIS Health 2008) showing the breadth and depth of their transparency.

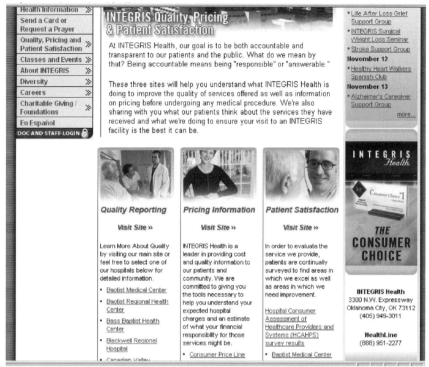

http://www.integris-health.com/INTEGRIS/en-US/Quality/default.htm

FIGURE 8.2
INTEGRIS website: Quality, pricing, and patient satisfaction.

BOARD QUESTIONS

As a hospital board member, consider these questions:

1. How does our organization compare on publicly reported indicators?
2. What are the next indicators to be publicly reported locally and nationally?
3. Are we publishing our own data on our website? Why or why not?
4. Are we educating staff well enough on these measures and our philosophy?
5. Are we educating the community on these publicly reported quality measures?

6. Are we transparent not just on data, but on key practices and policies, such as how we collect patient payments or how we communicate medical errors?

7. Is there important information we see in the Boardroom that members of the community would value or use for their care? Are we sharing this information with the community? Why or why not?

REFERENCES

Baily, M. N., and R. E. Litan. *A Brief Guide to Fixing Finance.* Washington, DC: The Brookings Institution, 2008, http://www.brookings.edu/papers/2008/0922_fixing_finance_baily_litan.aspx (accessed November 2, 2008).

Gelinas, L. S., and D. Y.-H. Loh. "The Effect of Workforce Issues on Patient Safety." *Nurs Econ* 22, no. 5 (2004): 266–272.

Hibbard, J. H., J. Stockard, and M. Tusler. "Does Publicizing Hospital Performance Stimulate Quality Improvement Efforts?" *Health Aff (Millwood)* 22, no. 2 (2003): 84–94.

INTEGRIS Health. *INTEGRIS Quality, Pricing, and Patient Satisfaction.* 2008, http://www.integris-health.com/INTEGRIS/en-US/Quality/default.htm (accessed November 9, 2008).

Kaiser Family Foundation (KFF), Agency for Healthcare Research and Quality (AHRQ), and Harvard School of Public Health. *National Survey on Consumers' Experiences with Patient Safety and Quality Information.* 2004, http://www.ahrq.gov/qual/consattitud.htm (accessed November 2, 2008).

Klein, S. "In Focus: Paying Attention to Performance Data." *Quality Matters* November/December, 2007, http://www.commonwealthfund.org/qualitymatters/qualitymatters_list.htm?issue_id=3735 (accessed November 5, 2008).

Kroszner, R. S. "Prospects for Recovery and Repair of Mortgage Markets." Presented at the annual conference of State Bank Supervisors, Amelia Island, Plantation, FL, May 22, 2008, http://www.federalreserve.gov/newsevents/speech/kroszner20080522a.htm (accessed November 2, 2008).

Norton Healthcare. *Norton Quality Report.* 2008, http://www.nortonhealthcare.com/about/qualityreport/index.aspx (accessed November 4, 2008).

Schneider, E. C., and T. Lieberman. "Publicly Disclosed Information about the Quality of Health Care: Response of the U.S. Public." *Qual Health Care* 10, no. 2 (2001): 96–103.

Schoen, C., S. K. How, I. Weinbaum, J. E. Craig, Jr., and K. Davis. *Public Views on Shaping the Future of the U. S. Health System.* New York: Commonwealth Fund, 2006, http://www.commonwealthfund.org/publications/publications_show.htm?doc_id=394606 (accessed November 4, 2008).

9

Healthcare Transformer 3: Payment Reform

A growing number of programs in the United States are testing different payment systems. Many of these programs are called pay-for-performance (P4P) to reflect the linkage of payment tied to performance levels. Healthcare Transformer 3, payment reform (see Figure 9.1), includes both P4P and other fundamental payment models that have yet to be tested on a broad scale but are quickly emerging. Designing, implementing, and learning from P4P and other payment reform programs are instrumental to fundamentally changing the vast and increasing financial facet of healthcare.

FIGURE 9.1
Top Ten Healthcare Transformers.

PROBLEM

The American healthcare system is primarily a transaction-based payment system. Such a system is predicated on payment linked to volume of services—generally, the more you do, the more money you receive. Fixed prices or payments are, of course, very common in the hospital setting, with the use of diagnosis-related groups (DRGs) for payment. However, the current payment system is largely built on a fee-for-service (FFS) platform.

One distinct characteristic of the American healthcare reimbursement system is its incredible complexity. Providers may be reimbursed by:

- FFS, or receiving a differential fee based on the service
- Capitation, or physicians receiving a fixed fee for a patient
- Per diem, or a hospital receiving a daily rate for a patient
- Case rate, or a hospital receiving a rate based on a specific patient diagnosis

All of these payment models may be adjusted based on other factors, such as the severity of the patient case, the type of hospital (teaching or nonteaching), or the market. Results from a survey of national opinion leaders showed that FFS payment—the most prevalent system in the United States—is "not effective in encouraging efficient, high-quality health care" (Stremikis, Guterman, and Davis 2008).

Regardless of the payment mechanism, the financial impact is tremendous. The chart in Figure 9.2 shows the comparison of the United States to other countries on healthcare spending. The United States spends almost 15% of the gross domestic product (GDP) on healthcare, 50% more than other advanced, industrialized countries such as Germany, Canada, France, Australia, and the United Kingdom.

However, not only does U.S. healthcare cost more in absolute dollars than in other countries, the rate of increase in health insurance premiums has far outpaced overall inflation and workers' earnings. As seen in Figure 9.3, for the last decade, health insurance premiums have increased 5–14% annually on average, whereas inflation has increased by 2–4% each year. The current, complicated payment system has resulted in incredible total costs to the United States and is unsustainable for the future.

Over the last few years, P4P programs have grown exponentially: there are more than 100 different programs in the country (Baker and Carter

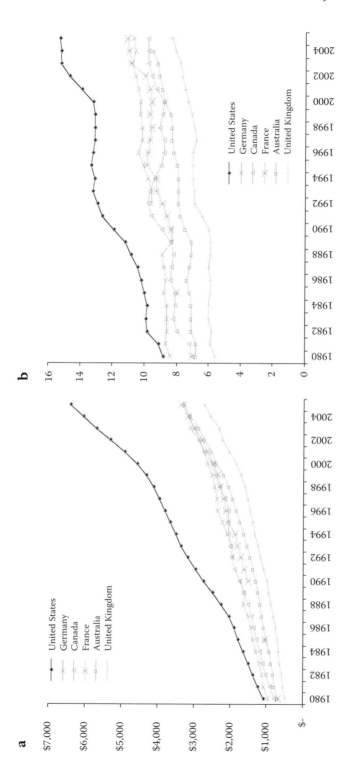

FIGURE 9.2

International comparison of spending on health, 1980–2005. a. Average spending on health per capita ($US purchasing power parity). b. Total expenditures on health as percent of GDP. (From Commonwealth Fund. *Why Not the Best? National Scorecard on U.S. Health System Performance, 2008.* With permission.)

Data: OECD Health Data 2007, Version 10/2007.

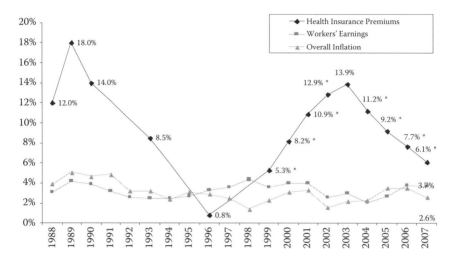

FIGURE 9.3

Average percentage increase in health insurance premiums compared to other indicators, 1988–2007. (From Kaiser Family Foundation and Health Research & Educational Trust. *Employer Health Benefits: 2008 Annual Survey.* With permission.) KPMG Survey of Employer-Sponsored Health Benefits, 1993, 1996; The Health Insurance Association of America (HIAA), 1988, 1989, 1990; Bureau of Labor Statistics, Consumer Price Index, U.S. City Average of Annual Inflation (April to April), 1988–2007; Bureau of Labor Statistics, Seasonally Adjusted Data from the Current Employment Statistics Survey, 1988–2007 (April to April).

*Estimate is statistically different from estimate for the previous year shown ($P < .05$). No statistical tests are conducted for years prior to 1999.

Note: Data on premium increases reflect the cost of health insurance premiums for a family of four. The average premium increase is weighted by covered workers.

2004). With so many programs, it may be surprising to note that there are few well-designed studies evaluating the impact of P4P programs on improved health. The message from the limited studies is mixed in terms of the relationship of P4P programs to better health outcomes. The greatest challenge is identifying the effect of P4P programs by themselves because P4P is often utilized along with other quality improvement strategies (such as public reporting or quality improvement assistance).

TRANSFORMER

Reforming the payment system is not a panacea to improved healthcare; however, it is necessary. The healthcare executive's approach to payment reform must include four major elements:

1. Assess: The current misaligned payment system needs to change. It is imperative to assess where the current payment system falls short or even has perverse incentives to "do the wrong thing." Identify areas where improved quality could negatively affect financial health. Consider how your organization can mitigate these areas or acknowledge them and continue forward with quality improvement.
2. Evaluate: With the glut of payment redesign programs, the organization must evaluate the potential impact of different programs on the financial bottom line. Through simulation of data or scenario planning, calculating how various programs will affect the organization is useful in identifying opportunities for improvement.
3. Design and test: Considering the assessment and evaluation, design payment reform models that reflect your improvement opportunities and priorities. It is important to recognize that no perfect system can be designed; focus rather on developing a system that is simple and easy to understand and set up to test specific elements of payment reform.
4. Learn: In today's environment, payment reform can be considered experimental. We do not know the best answer or have the clear methods to get there. However, we can design multiple experiments well so that we can learn and improve on them. A critical component of payment reform design and implementation, learning is essential in transformation.

BEST PRACTICES

The intersection of quality and cost is most evident in the Centers for Medicare and Medicaid Services/Premier Hospital Quality Incentive Demonstration project. More than 250 hospitals participated in this national demonstration project in which hospitals received financial rewards and public recognition for high performance in several quality measures. Thirty-three measures from five clinical conditions (pneumonia, coronary artery bypass graft, acute myocardial infarction, hip and knee replacement procedures, and heart failure) were evaluated over time. Participating hospitals were provided the results of these measures using common definitions and the quality scores were publicly reported. Hospitals were also provided financial rewards on the basis of their performance ranking. In year 3 of the project, 112 hospitals received more than $7 million in total incentive payments (Premier 2008). In terms of quality, the composite quality score (which is an aggregation of all of the clinical measures) improved by 4.4% from year 2 to year 3 and increased by nearly 16% over the project's 3 years. The findings from this P4P project are profound and clear: these types of programs have the potential to improve clinical quality, save lives, and reduce costs (Remus 2006). In the project, when pneumonia, coronary artery bypass graft, acute myocardial infarction, and hip/knee patients received most or all of the interventions they were eligible for, they had better outcomes, shorter lengths of stay, and lower costs.

The Network for Regional Healthcare Improvement (NRHI) has produced a primer on healthcare payment reform and developed recommendations based on the discussion of leading national and regional experts and stakeholders. Several recommendations are essential to provider organizations furthering payment and quality reform (NRHI 2008). The recommendations center on the concepts of how to:

- Encourage use of higher value providers and services
- Protect patients in new payment systems
- Pilot new payment systems
- Encourage payers and providers to support new payment systems
- Identify and use community-wide structures to support payment reform

A major reform effort is focused on bundled payments—combining payments to doctors, hospitals, and post-acute providers into one single, combined payment to cover a patient's complete case. NRHI (2008) also issued the following set of important recommendations related to provider organizational structures needed to manage bundled payments:

A true episode-of-care payment system for major acute care involves paying a single price for all services delivered by all providers involved in a patient's care. But combining the services of hospitals, physicians, and post-acute care providers into a single payment—called "bundling" the payment—presumes the existence of an entity that can serve as the recipient of the single payment and divide it among the individual providers in a manner acceptable to those providers. Episode-of-care payment also envisions the provision of warranties—commitments by healthcare providers to address errors or complications without charging for additional services—but this increases the challenges associated with bundled payments because of the difficulties of apportioning responsibility for the errors or complications among the multiple providers involved. What kinds of organizational structures can support payment bundling, and how can both payment systems and healthcare organizations evolve to achieve these goals? The following are core recommendations:

Recommendation: Payers should make bundled payments to provider organizations and partnerships that demonstrate the capacity and expertise to manage the full episode of care and the associated payments.

Recommendation: Payers, providers, regional collaboratives, and other organizations should take steps to facilitate the transition to bundled payments, including public reporting about the total costs of care, providing technical assistance to providers, and making transitional changes to payment systems.

Recommendation: Restrictions on providers' ability to divide bundled payments among themselves should provide an appropriate balance between protecting patients and encouraging innovation, and should ensure a level playing field for negotiations among providers. (NRHI 2008, Reprinted with permission from Harold Miller and NRHI)

BOARD QUESTIONS

As a board member, consider these questions:

1. How will the organization's bottom line be affected by Medicare payment reform programs? By Medicaid? By the different commercial models?

2. Are we planning and implementing payment reform within our health system?

3. What have we learned from different P4P programs?

4. How are we encouraging providers to test payment reform systems?

5. How would we effectively implement a bundled payment system in our health system community?

6. How are we communicating payment reform models to our staff, patients, and community?

7. If bundled payments were implemented, is our hospital system capable of administering a bundled payment program across all services?

8. If bundled payments were implemented, is our hospital system capable of managing patients across the full spectrum of care (ambulatory care, inpatient care, home care, and other institutional and ancillary care)?

REFERENCES

Baker, G., and B. Carter. "The Evolution of Pay-for-Performance Models for Rewarding Providers," in *Case Studies in Health Plan Pay-for-Performance.* Washington, DC: Atlantic Information Services, 2004.

Commonwealth Fund. *Why Not the Best? National Scorecard on U.S. Health System Performance, 2008.* 2008, http://www.commonwealthfund.org/chartcartcharts/chartcartcharts_show.htm?doc_id=694013&attrib_id=14492 (accessed November 2, 2008).

Kaiser Family Foundation and Health Research & Educational Trust. *Employer Health Benefits: 2008 Annual Survey.* 2008, http://www.kff.org/insurance/7790/ (accessed November 2, 2008).

Network for Regional Healthcare Improvement (NRHI). *Executive Summary. From Volume to Value: Transforming Healthcare Payment and Delivery Systems to Improve Quality and Reduce Costs. Recommendations of the 2008 NRHI Healthcare Payment Reform Summit.* 2008, http://www.nrhi.org (accessed November 2, 2008).

Premier. *CMS/Premier Hospital Quality Incentive Demonstration (HQID).* 2008, http://www.premierinc.com/quality-safety/tools-services/p4p/hqi/index.jsp (accessed November 16, 2008).

Remus, D. *Exploring the Nexus of Quality and Cost.* Charlotte, NC: Premier, Inc., 2006.

Stremikis, K., S. Guterman, and K. Davis. *Health Care Opinion Leaders' Views on Payment System Reform.* New York: Commonwealth Fund, 2008.

10

Healthcare Transformer 2: Culture

Culture is the most often spoken barrier to improving healthcare and, yet, perhaps the least understood. Culture is the way things are done in an organization and are reflective of behaviors, norms, and beliefs. Healthcare transformation will not occur unless the culture of the industry and healthcare organizations also transforms (see Figure 10.1). An often quoted phrase is that "culture eats strategy for lunch," symbolizing that all change plans are meaningless if they counter the prevailing cultural norm. Dramatic change starts, includes, and ends with culture.

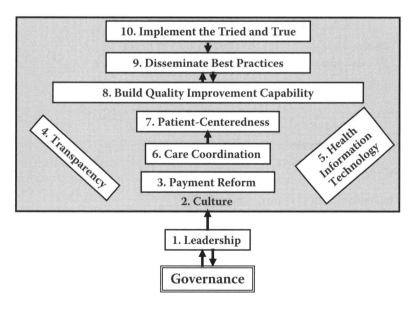

FIGURE 10.1
Top Ten Healthcare Transformers.

PROBLEM

The lack of positive (open, "no-blame") culture is extremely detrimental to quality of care and patient safety, as seen in the following classic studies:

- Between 50% and 96% of adverse events are not reported, largely because of a culture of fear (Barach and Small 2000; Leape 1994).
- Approximately 55% of organizations reported that organization culture (i.e., hierarchy and intimidation, failure to function as a team, and failure to follow the chain of communication) was a root cause in infant death and injury (Joint Commission 2004).

Recently, MacDavitt, Chou, and Stone (2007) in an extensive literature review identified the importance of culture and organizational climate in studies that showed:

- Leadership, group behavior (coordination and communication), and conflict management were directly associated with employee satisfaction, lower nurse turnover, and higher perceived quality of patient care.
- Leadership (safety climate characterized by safety procedure, flow of safety information, and organizational priority of safety) was associated with higher rates of treatment error reports.
- Nurse-physician relationships were associated with lower mortality rates.

TRANSFORMER

The transformer opportunity includes:

1. Quality and safety as a top priority: This requires that quality and safety is
   - A major goal in the strategic plan
   - An agenda item at all board and management meetings
   - Monitored on an ongoing basis through specific measures

- A major factor in the performance evaluation of managers and staff (accountability)
2. Values: Organizations must formally state, emphasize, and practice values that facilitate quality and safety. The five most important are:
   - Open flow of information and communication
   - A learning organization which proactively assesses risks, provides continual feedback on quality information, learns from mistakes and best practices, and makes improvements
   - Systems thinking—looking at underlying issues (communication, staffing, resources, lack of effective processes) that cause quality and safety issues
   - "No blame" culture where individuals feel free to speak out and identify and report problems
   - Collaboration and coordination among individuals, units, departments, and settings of care
3. Leadership: Key leadership actions to create a positive culture include
   - Modeling the values identified above
   - Ongoing emphasis on quality and safety in management rounds and meetings
   - Being open to staff suggestions to improve patient safety
   - Continually looking for and addressing systems problems that could affect quality and patient safety
4. Policies, systems, and procedures: The following mechanisms should be put into place:
   - A policy on a fair and just culture (first examining systems problems, but having accountability for reckless, willful, or negligent behavior)
   - A system to report medical errors that is easy to use and nonpunitive
   - Meetings in which errors and near misses are openly discussed and solutions found
5. Teamwork: This includes training to develop skills in
   - Conflict management and decision-making
   - Patient "handoffs"
   - Interpersonal communication
   - Methods for interdisciplinary coordination
   - Ground rules for teamwork (mutual respect, listening to others, providing constructive input)

BEST PRACTICES

The following are practices that have been shown to create a positive organizational culture or climate for quality and patient safety:

- Delineation of patient safety priorities: Organizations should clearly specify their priorities in patient safety to motivate staff and target improvement efforts. For example, Ascension Health has identified the following patient safety priorities:
  - Joint Commission National Patient Safety Goals
  - Preventable mortality
  - Adverse drug events
  - Falls
  - Pressure ulcers
  - Surgical complications
  - Nosocomial infections
  - Perinatal safety (Pryor et al. 2006)
- Hospital survey on patient safety culture: The Agency for Healthcare Research and Quality (AHRQ) has developed surveys that allow organizations to assess such critical variables affecting culture as communication, supervision, and willingness to report medical errors (AHRQ 2008). This allows your organization to be compared with others so that you can examine the effectiveness of your cultural change efforts. The survey can be found at http://www.ahrq. gov/qual/hospculture/hospform.pdf.
- Fair and Just culture: The Dana Farber Cancer Institute (DFCI) has included individual accountability in its patient safety culture. DFCI has a policy that states:

> A fair and just culture means giving constructive feedback and critical analysis in skillful ways, doing assessments that are based on facts, and having respect for the complexity of the situation. It also means providing fair-minded treatment, having productive conversations, and creating effective structures that help people reveal their errors and help the organization learn from them...
>
> DFCI commits to holding individuals accountable for their own performance in accordance with their job responsibilities and the DFCI core values. However, individuals should not carry the burden for system flows over which they had no control. (Conner et al. 2007)

- Medical team training: Many hospitals have instituted Crew Resource Management (CRM) training. As mentioned in an earlier chapter, CRM originated from the aviation industry. It is interactive training and team building in such areas as structured communication approaches, assertiveness, and ground rules for teamwork and collaboration (Dunn et al. 2007).
- Communication mechanisms: The VA National Center for Patient Safety (NCPS) has developed and implemented in VA facilities several effective interventions to improve communication and coordination to address quality and patient safety issues, including:
  - Briefings and debriefings by surgical teams
  - Interdisciplinary patient-centered rounds in the ICU
  - A standardized process for transferring patient care responsibilities
  - Debriefings of cardio-pulmonary resuscitation events
  - Interdisciplinary administrative briefings and problem solving meetings in clinical units (Falzetta, Robinson, and Dunn 2007)
- "Near miss" meetings: This meeting or an agenda item at a quality improvement or staff meeting is designed to be a no-blame, open discussion of errors that were caught or nearly made. A quality professional or a designated person on the unit or service usually facilitates this meeting. Individuals are encouraged and even rewarded for identifying the near miss, and a discussion ensues on ways to prevent the potential error in the future.
- Nonpunitive reporting: Upstate Medical University Hospital (UMUH) in Syracuse, New York, instituted a confidential reporting system for medication errors to address the problem of the underreporting of errors. The medical occurrence (error) report form was revised so that the person who committed or discovered the error would not be identified. The reports were submitted to an interdisciplinary team (nurse, physician, and pharmacist) that studied the incident and instituted process improvements to prevent similar occurrences. The results in identifying medical errors were remarkable, as seen by the average number of reports per month that increased from 19 to 102 (Lehmann et al. 2007).
- Comprehensive organization development: Johns Hopkins Hospital instituted a Comprehensive Unit-Based Safety Program (CUSP) to improve quality, safety, and communication in their intensive care through the use of eight steps.

Assessment of the unit's culture of safety:

1. Education of staff on the sciences of safety (e.g., anatomy of errors, systems thinking, interpersonal skills, blame versus responsibility)
2. Identification of safety concerns
3. Meeting regularly with a senior hospital executive who "adopts" the unit to provide support for removing system barriers and accountability for making safety improvements
4. Prioritization of improvements
5. Making the improvements
6. Sharing of success stories and disseminating results
7. Reassessment of the unit's safety culture

The results were extremely positive in the two study sites: the oncology surgical ICU (known as the Weinberg ICU or WICU) and the surgical ICU (SICU):

- The length of stay decreased from 2 days to 1 day in WICU and from 3 days to 2 days in the SICU.
- In both the WICU and SICU, catheter-related bloodstream infections were eliminated, preventing an estimated 43 infections and eight deaths.
- Staff ratings of a positive safety culture increased from 35% to 52% in the WICU and from 35% to 68% in the SICU (Commonwealth Fund 2008).

BOARD QUESTIONS

As a hospital board member, consider these questions:

1. Is a culture of quality and patient safety a strategic goal for the organization?
2. Have we defined our desired culture of high performance?
3. Have measures and goals of a desired culture been delineated for the organization?
4. Are we evaluating responses to culture surveys by physicians, nurses, and administrators to assess differences?

5. What are the top cultural changes we are trying to change and how?
6. How are we strategically and tactically trying to improve teamwork?
7. Are there clear and stated values that facilitate an open, trusting, and learning culture in the organization?

REFERENCES

Agency for Healthcare Research and Quality (AHRQ). *Patient Safety Culture Surveys.* 2008, http://www.ahrq.gov/qual/hospculture/ (accessed November 20, 2008).

Barach, P., and S. Small. "Reporting and Preventing Medical Mishaps: Lessons from Non-Medical Near Miss Reporting Systems." *Br Med J* 320 (2000): 759–763.

Commonwealth Fund. *Case Study: Adopting a Comprehensive, Unit-Based Approach to Patient Safety at Johns Hopkins Hospital.* 2008, http://www.commonwealthfund.org/innovations/innovations_show.htm?doc_id=707926 (accessed November 20, 2008).

Conner, M., D. Duncombe, E. Barclay, S. Bartel, E. Gross, C. Miller, and P. Reid Ponte. "Creating a Fair and Just Culture: One Institution's Path toward Organizational Change." *Jt Comm J Qual Patient Saf* 33 (2007): 617–624.

Dunn, E., P. Mills, J. Neily, M. Crittenden, A. Carmack, and J. Bagian. "Medical Team Training: Applying Crew Resource Management in the Veterans Health Administration." *Jt Comm J Qual Patient Saf* 33 (2007): 317–325.

Falzetta, L., A. Carmack, L. Robinson, and E. Dunn. "Improving Communication in Healthcare." *Patient Safety & Quality Healthcare* 5, no. 1 (2007): 18–20.

Joint Commission. *Sentinel Event Alert Issue #30.* 2004, http://www.jointcommission.org/SentinelEvents/SentinelEventAlert/sea_30.htm (accessed November 20, 2008).

Leape, L. "Error in Medicine." *J Am Med Assoc* 272 (1994): 1151–1157.

Lehmann, D., N. Page, K. Kirschman, A. Sedore, R. Guharoy, J. Medicis, R. Ploudtz-Snyder, R. Weinstock, and D. Duggan. "Every Error a Treasure: Improving Medication Use with a Nonpunitive Reporting System." *Jt Comm J Qual Patient Saf* 33 (2007): 401–407.

MacDavitt, K., S. Chou, and P. Stone. "Organizational Climate and Health Care Outcomes." *Jt Comm J Qual Patient Saf* 33, Suppl. 11 (2007): 45–56.

Pryor, D. B., S. Tolchin, A. Hendrich, C. Thomas, and A. Tersigni. "The Clinical Transformation of Ascension Health: Eliminating All Preventable Injuries and Deaths." *Jt Comm J Qual Patient Saf* 32 (2006): 299–308.

11

Healthcare Transformer 1: Leadership

Leadership is the key to organizational performance and thus appropriately identified as Transformer 1 in Figure 11.1. Leaders can drive *transformational change*—that is, changes in values and patterns of behavior so that healthcare organizations can address long-standing performance and quality issues. Effective leadership is a foundational lever for dramatically improving the performance of an organization and cumulatively, the industry. The Baldrige National Quality Program, in its healthcare criteria for performance excellence, identifies leadership as its first criterion and states that leaders should set organizational vision and values, create a sustainable organization, and promote a culture of patient safety (NIST 2008).

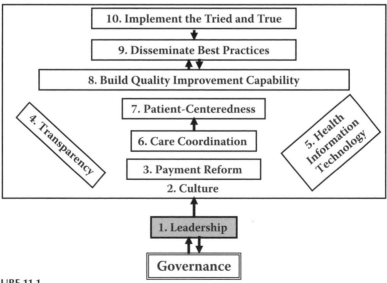

FIGURE 11.1
Top Ten Healthcare Transformers.

PROBLEM

The need for leadership to transform healthcare systems can be seen in the following:

- As identified earlier, the Institute of Medicine (IOM) has stated that between 44,000 and 98,000 people die each year because of medical error (IOM 2000).
- Progress to address medical errors has been slow. The *2007 National Healthcare Quality Report* found that patient safety in U.S. healthcare organizations only improved by an annual rate of 1% (Clancy 2008).
- More recently a study in the *New England Journal of Medicine* showed that only 67% of patients said that they would definitely recommend the hospital in which they received care (Jha et al. 2008).
- Most medical errors are caused not by individual incompetence but by poor systems and processes that are under the control of leaders throughout the organization. In his classic book, *Out of the Crisis*, Deming says, "Workers work in the system. Leaders work on the system." (Deming 1986).

TRANSFORMER

One excellent model of transformational leadership is provided by the Institute for Healthcare Improvement and Jim Reinersten, who state that leadership is a complex set of five interrelated activities as shown in Figure 11.2:

1. Set direction: The leader's job is to set the "future self-image" of the organization. This task can be described as creating a magnetic field whereby all members are both pulled (attracted) toward a positive future or pushed out (repelled) of status quo.

2. Establish the foundation: The foundation starts with leaders preparing themselves. It then builds with the education of their subordinates and teams with knowledge and skills to improve healthcare

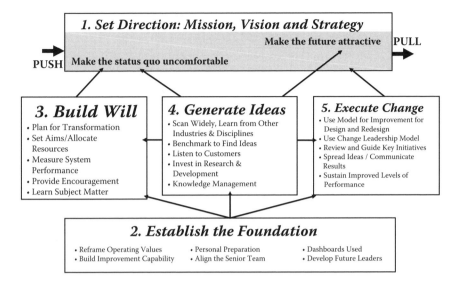

FIGURE 11.2
IHI/Reinertsen leadership model. (From Reinertsen J.L., M. Bisognano, M.D. Pugh. *Seven Leadership Leverage Points for Organization-Level Improvement in Health Care (Second Edition).* IHI Innovation Series White Paper. Cambridge, MA: Institute for Healthcare Improvement; 2008. With permission.)

systems and manage the change process. In addition, leaders must establish the values and practices necessary to ensure quality and patient safety.

3. Build will: Leaders must overcome the comfort of the status quo and build commitment to a new culture of quality improvement and patient safety. Ways to do this include emphasizing quality at all management meetings, showing the business case (financial benefits) of improvement initiatives, having incentives for quality improvements, and holding all leaders accountable for making the transformation.

4. Generate ideas: Innovation is necessary to address quality and safety issues. Effective leaders look for ideas and best practices from other organizations and the literature. They also have mechanisms to solicit ideas from their staff. These ideas and practices (whether from external or internal sources) are rapidly tested and adapted/implemented as appropriate.

5. Execute change: Leaders should use and promulgate a clear model for improvement design and redesign such as the Plan-Do-Study-Act cycle, ensure that lessons learned from improvement projects get disseminated in the organization, have a clear performance metric to assess the effectiveness of change efforts, and reinforce that continuous quality improvement is everyone's job in the organization (Reinersten 2008).

BEST PRACTICES

The following are practices that have been shown to create a positive organizational culture or climate for quality and patient safety:

- Role of the chief executive officer (CEO): Dr. William Rupp, who served as both board chairman and CEO of Luther Midelfort–Mayo Health System (LM) in Eau Claire, Wisconsin, is quoted below regarding the roles of the CEO in providing leadership for quality.
  1. The CEO must always be strategically **searching for the next good idea**. On my own, I come up with maybe one good idea every two or three years. But I can recognize someone else's good idea in a flash, and my organization can get that idea implemented.
  2. **The CEO must push the quality agenda.** He or she must be seen to be in charge of it and must make it happen. There are many forces lined up to preserve the status quo, and if the CEO doesn't visibly lead quality, the necessary changes won't happen.
  3. The CEO doesn't make change happen single-handedly. The leader does so **through key change agents**, and his or her job is to protect and support those change agents, while listening carefully to the pain they cause.
  4. The whole experience has profoundly reinforced for me the concept of a **system of quality**. The professional culture that focuses responsibility for quality and safety solely on individuals is dead wrong. The vast majority of our staff is doing the best they can. Asking them to, "Think harder next time," or telling, "Don't ever do that again," will not work (Reinersten 2008).
- Board involvement and transparency: INTEGRIS Health, a large

not-for-profit health system in Oklahoma, has established a systematic, board-led approach to quality improvement. Key elements of approach include:

1. Having a quality review committee at each hospital board.
2. Starting every hospital board meeting with quality as its first agenda item.
3. Establishing a chairperson's council on quality that consists of board chairpersons, chiefs of staff, and executives from every INTEGRIS facility.
4. Identifying the following as key areas of focus: system performance on clinical process and outcomes measures, patient perceptions of care, and public reporting.
5. Making hospital performance transparent to patients and the public by providing data on quality, patient satisfaction, and prices for services on the INTEGRIS website (Dragoo and Bethea 2007).

- System redesign—leadership guidelines: In a study of 16 healthcare providers, the following were identified as the four critical success factors that lead to effective system redesign to improve quality:

1. Involving all leaders
2. Strategically aligning and integrating improvement efforts with organizational priorities
3. Systematically establishing infrastructure, process, and performance appraisal systems for continuous improvement
4. Actively developing champions, teams, and staff (Wang et al. 2006)

- System redesign—specific leadership interventions: Sentara Health, a large not-for-profit system in Virginia, has implemented the following strategies to improve the reliability of the system for quality and patient safety:

1. Simplifying work processes, which can reduce the number of serious adverse events.
2. Using daily "check-ins," which are short, focused meetings of leaders and staff from each unit to provide information and discuss any systems issues that could affect patient care.
3. Conducting "executive rounds" in which senior leaders emphasize safety, model desired behaviors, allow staff to identify issues, and then follow up on identified issues.

4. Having "huddles" in every unit every 12 hours whereby staff can identify and discuss any safety issue, including any concerns about workload and staffing.
5. Establishing a performance management system whereby staff is held accountable for results and rewards are provided as appropriate (Hines et al. 2008).

BOARD QUESTIONS

As a hospital board member, consider these questions:

1. Is quality a strategic imperative and a specific agenda item at each board meeting?
2. Are there mechanisms for innovation, particularly for staff, to identify ideas that would address quality and patient safety issues?
3. Are leaders being held accountable for quality measures and are they rewarded when improvements have been made?
4. Have patient safety priorities been delineated for your organization?
5. Are there programs in place to develop leaders and staff in quality improvement?
6. Is leadership actively engaged in the organization's quality improvement strategy?
7. Are there specific interventions in place to improve the reliability of the system such as simplifying work processes, daily check-ins, huddles, and executive rounds?
8. Do you expect leadership to possess the same experience and expertise in quality as compared to finance?
9. Do you hold leadership accountable for quality performance at the same level as financial performance?

REFERENCES

Clancy, C. C. "Putting Reliability into Practice: Lessons from Healthcare Leaders." *Patient Safety and Quality Healthcare* 5 (May–June 2008): 6-7.
Deming, W. E. *Out of the Crisis.* Cambridge, MA: MIT Press, 1986.

Dragoo, S. D., and D. F. Bethea. "INTEGRIS Baptist Medical Center: Transparency and Returnship Take Quality to the Community." *Jt Comm J Qual Patient Saf* 33 (2008): 596–600.

Hines, S., K. Luna, J. Lofthus, M. Marquardt, and D. Stelmokas. *Becoming a High Reliability Organization: Operational Advice for Hospital Leaders.* Prepared by the Lewin Group under Contract No. 290-04-0011 for the Agency for Healthcare Research and Quality, AHRQ Publication No. 080-0022, 2008, http://www.ahrq.gov/qual/hroadvice/hroadvice.pdf (accessed November 1, 2008)

Jha, A. K., E. J. Orav, J. Zheng, and A. M. Epstein. "Patients' Perceptions of Hospital Care in the United States." *New Engl J Med* 359 (2008): 1921–1931.

National Institute of Standards and Technology (NIST). *Baldrige National Quality Program: Health Care Criteria for Performance Excellence.* 2008, http://www.baldrige.gov/PDF_files/2008_HealthCare_Criteria.pdf (accessed November 1, 2008).

Reinertsen, J. L. "Leadership for Quality," in *The Healthcare Quality Book.* Edited by S. B. Ransom, M. S. Joshi, and D. B. Nash, 309–328, Chicago: Health Administration Press, 2008.

Reinertsen J.L., M. Bisognano, M.D. Pugh. *Seven Leadership Leverage Points for Organization-Level Improvement in Health Care (Second Edition).* IHI Innovation Series White Paper. Cambridge, MA: Institute for Healthcare Improvement; 2008. Available on www.IHI. org.

Wang, M. C., J. K. Hyun, J. I. Harrison, S. M. Shortell, and I. Fraser. "Redesigning Health Systems for Quality: Lessons from Emerging Practices." *Jt Comm J Qual Patient Saf* 32 (2006): 599–611.

12

Conclusion: The Governance Engagement Checklist

Governance is the foundation of the Top Ten Healthcare Transformers model (see Figure 12.1). The board of trustees or directors governs the organization and has the fiduciary responsibility to carry out the mission of the organization. As can be seen from the model, governance's direct relationship with leadership is the basis for the effective and efficient implementation of the healthcare transformers. In that realm, the engagement of the board in transforming the organization is essential.

Governance engagement may be categorized into three major areas that serve as the pillars for the board to be involved in the transformation agenda set forth in this book:

FIGURE 12.1
Top Ten Healthcare Transformers.

1. Increasing the quality literacy of the board
2. Establishing a clear agenda for quality and transformation and aligning that agenda with the overall organizational plan
3. Leveraging patient input and transparency to become patient-centered (Joshi and Hines 2006)

QUALITY LITERACY

Quality is a complex topic that requires tremendous time and attention to understand well. Education of board members and chief executive officers is warranted, particularly about the broad transformational issues that are called for in this book. There are many ways to achieve this, such as conducting retreats focused on quality and sending board members to quality conferences. Additionally, hospitals should consider recruiting board members with expertise in quality. A component of literacy is also developing a questioning mindset. An important question to pose regularly is "Are we moving fast enough in improving?"

AGENDA AND ALIGNMENT

Transformation does not happen by chance and requires setting an agenda for transformation that builds sufficient time for discussion and open dialogue. Specific to the agenda, time must be allocated to defining bold aims with clear goals and timelines, thereby developing a strategy map that demonstrates a clear, strategic, and operational linkage between projects, strategies, and measurable goals. Finally, these important elements must be monitored, and leadership must be held accountable for their implementation.

PATIENT-CENTEREDNESS

Patient-centeredness, as noted as a healthcare transformer, can be greatly elevated by three key governance actions. The first is to have the board listen to patient stories of medical errors or near misses to identify system-level improvements. The second is to ensure that the hospital has a system in place to involve patients and families in performance improvement. Finally, by being transparent with the community (local, peer, and provider communities), all stakeholders are placed on the same level, which can propel an organization from defending its performance to opening up and accelerating its performance improvement. Figure 12.2 summarizes the key elements into a governance checklist.

The same governance checklist can be reformatted as a graph (see Figure 12.3) to show how a board of directors can move along these three major pillars. As seen in the bar diagram, to move up the quality literacy pillar, a board will start with awareness of the issues and move toward education, dialogue, and expertise. To move up the agenda/alignment pillar, the board will move from setting aims to monitoring a measurable strategic and operating plan to hardwiring accountability. To move up the patient-centeredness pillar, the board will move from capturing patient input to patient involvement to being transparent on performance.

As a hospital board member and leader, use the individual healthcare transformer chapters, this governance engagement checklist, and the appendix that compiles all of the board questions. The board questions are

Quality Literacy
- Conduct ongoing education on salient quality issues
- Continuously question the pace of improvement in the organization
- Ensure that expertise in healthcare quality, patient safety, and transformational change is present on the board

Agenda and Alignment
- Devote sufficient time on the agenda for quality and have open dialogue on the agenda for emerging quality issues
- Set bold aims that articulate clear goals with clear dates
- Effectively monitor system-level performance
- Align the quality plan with the overall organizational strategic plan
- Develop and monitor a strategy map that links key projects to strategic drivers to measures and goals
- Set financial incentives for leadership on the basis of overall quality goals

Patient-Centeredness
- Have patients and families share stories to serve as an input for board agenda-setting
- Involve patients and families in improvement initiatives
- Be transparent with the community on performance

FIGURE 12.2
Governance engagement checklist.

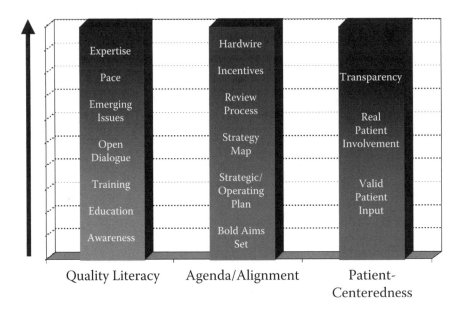

FIGURE 12.3
Governance engagement.

the basis for having an open and honest dialogue that welcomes questioning, debate, and knowledge. A board culture that embraces these values and behaviors will lead to healthcare transformation.

REFERENCES

Alexander, J. A., and S. D. Lee. "Does Governance Matter? Board Configuration and Performance in Not-for-Profit Hospitals." *Milbank Q* 84, no. 4 (2006): 733–758.

Bisognano, M., J. McCannon, and L. Botwinick. "A Campaign to Save 100,000 Lives." *Trustee* 58, no. 8 (2005): 1, 12–14, 19.

Joshi, M., and S. Hines. "Getting the Board on Board: Engaging Hospital Boards in Quality and Patient Safety." *Jt Comm J Qual Patient Saf* 32, no. 4 (2006): 179–187.

Kroch, E., T. Vaughn, M. Koepke, S. Roman, D. Foster, S. Sinha, and S. Levey. "Hospital Boards and Quality Dashboards." *J Patient Saf* 2, no. 1 (2006): 10–19.

Kurtzman, E., and C. Page-Lopez. *Hospital Governing Boards and Quality of Care: A Call to Responsibility.* Washington, DC: National Quality Forum, 2004.

Lockee, C., K. Kroom, E. Zablocki, and B. Bader. *Quality.* San Diego: The Governance Institute, 2006.

Appendix

This appendix compiles all of the "Board Questions" (over 80 questions) from Chapters 2 through 11 for each of the ten healthcare transformers.

RELIABLY IMPLEMENT THE TRIED AND TRUE—TRANSFORMER 10

1. How are we doing in implementing tried-and-true best practices? What are our results?
2. Have we implemented tried-and-true best practices of standing orders, clinical guidelines, and care bundles?
3. How do our results compare to (state and national) averages and to benchmarks?
4. Have we learned from the best-performing organizations that have achieved benchmark performance?
5. What do we still need to do to address any gaps between our current performance and the best?
6. What are the major lessons (successes and failures) from our recent quality improvement initiatives?
7. Have we "hardwired" (institutionalized and formalized) our processes for consistency and reliability?
8. Do we have the right systems and measures in place to track the sustaining of improved performance?
9. What are the nationally emerging best practices that we should be investigating and implementing?

DISSEMINATE BEST PRACTICES—TRANSFORMER 9

1. What best practices or improvement initiatives for dissemination should we focus on this year?
2. Is there a plan and mechanism in place to disseminate best practices?

3. What measures are we tracking to ensure effective dissemination of best practices?
4. What do the data show on the spread of our identified improvement efforts?
5. Are we identifying and leveraging early adopters and champions for leading the spread of best practices?
6. What are our biggest barriers to adoption of best practices, and what specific strategies are we using to overcome those barriers?
7. How are our leaders encouraged and incentivized to adopt best practices?
8. What strategies are we using to encourage an environment of dissemination and adoption?

BUILD ORGANIZATIONAL QUALITY IMPROVEMENT CAPABILITY—TRANSFORMER 8

1. Do I, as a board member, emphasize the importance of leadership in quality improvement and the need for quality improvement training?
2. Are there formal quality improvement training programs in the organization for (a) all managers, (b) team leaders, and (c) all employees?
3. How are we evaluating the training/development programs? How effective are they in changing attitudes, behaviors, skills, and results?
4. Are there mechanisms in place to track participation in training programs and performance in improving quality, patient safety, and patient satisfaction?
5. Are there succession plans to develop managers for higher levels of responsibility?
6. Is quality improvement a necessary competency for professional advancement and for leadership?

PATIENT-CENTEREDNESS—TRANSFORMER 7

1. How do we collect patient and family experience information for our planning and improvement?

2. How valid is our patient input?
3. Have we used one of the commonly available toolkits to perform an organizational assessment regarding patient-centeredness?
4. What are our biggest gaps and improvement opportunities in patient-centeredness?
5. How are we progressing toward patient-centeredness goals?
6. How are patients and families involved in the design of our improvement efforts?
7. How are patients and families engaged in their care?
8. Are we taking a more holistic view of healthcare by considering incorporation of features such as music, art, spiritual issues, and complementary medicine?
9. Are there evidenced-based patient-centered interventions that we should try implementing; for example, sharing patient stories of medical errors and near misses at board meetings, testing apologies, disclosures of errors, including patients on improvement teams, creating patient and family advisory councils, and making medical records more accessible to patients?
10. Are we measuring our organization's culture towards being more patient-centered?

CARE COORDINATION—TRANSFORMER 6

1. What measures are we using to track care coordination within the hospital and with other providers and stakeholders in the community and how are we doing?
2. Do I, as a board member, emphasize the importance of communication among providers within my organization and with referral providers and other entities that we interact with to ensure effective coordination and continuity of care?
3. Specifically, how do we ensure effective transitions and handoffs of information and care across shifts within the hospital?
4. Are there effective mechanisms in place for coordination within my organization such as joint rounding, OR briefings, case management, and discharge planning?
5. Are there effective mechanisms in place (e.g., use of patient liaisons) to assist patients in navigating the healthcare systems?

6. Am I advancing information management systems, particularly electronic health records, which would track and follow up on patient care needs?
7. Are we tracking our hospital's readmission rates?
8. Have we examined the main causes of avoidable readmissions and identified opportunities for improvement?
9. For factors that are outside of the hospital's control, are we working with community stakeholders to reduce avoidable readmissions?

HEALTH INFORMATION TECHNOLOGY— TRANSFORMER 5

1. What is our HIT strategic and operating plan?
2. Are we on track with the implementation of our various HIT systems?
3. What is our status in HIT implementation, specifically of CPOE systems, EHRs, and PHRs?
4. Is our HIT plan connecting partners in our community, that is, with other doctors, other healthcare providers, and other settings of care?
5. How are we encouraging greater use of PHRs?
6. Are we tracking and have we improved patient health outcomes and other key indicators as a result of HIT?
7. Are we measuring the cost-effectiveness of our HIT systems?
8. Are we constantly asking ourselves how we can leverage HIT to improve quality and safety?

TRANSPARENCY—TRANSFORMER 4

1. How does our organization compare on publicly reported indicators?
2. What are the next indicators to be publicly reported locally and nationally?
3. Are we publishing our own data on our website? Why or why not?
4. Are we educating staff well enough on these measures and our philosophy?
5. Are we educating the community on these publicly reported quality measures?

6. Are we transparent not just on data, but on key practices and policies, such as how we collect patient payments or how we communicate medical errors?

7. Is there important information we see in the Boardroom that members of the community would value or use for their care? Are we sharing this information with the community? Why or why not?

PAYMENT REFORM—TRANSFORMER 3

1. How will the organization's bottom line be affected by Medicare payment reform programs? By Medicaid? By the different commercial models?

2. Are we planning and implementing payment reform within our health system?

3. What have we learned from different P4P programs?

4. How are we encouraging providers to test payment reform systems?

5. How would we effectively implement a bundled payment system in our health system community?

6. How are we communicating payment reform models to our staff, patients, and community?

7. If bundled payments were implemented, is our hospital system capable of administering a bundled payment program across all services?

8. If bundled payments were implemented, is our hospital system capable of managing patients across the full spectrum of care (ambulatory care, inpatient care, home care, and other institutional and ancillary care)?

CULTURE—TRANSFORMER 2

1. Is a culture of quality and patient safety a strategic goal for the organization?

2. Have we defined our desired culture of high performance?

3. Have measures and goals of a desired culture been delineated for the organization?

4. Are we evaluating responses to culture surveys by physicians, nurses, and administrators to assess differences?
5. What are the top cultural changes we are trying to change and how?
6. How are we strategically and tactically trying to improve teamwork?
7. Are there clear and stated values that facilitate an open, trusting, and learning culture in the organization?

LEADERSHIP—TRANSFORMER 1

1. Is quality a strategic imperative and a specific agenda item at each board meeting?
2. Are there mechanisms for innovation, particularly for staff, to identify ideas that would address quality and patient safety issues?
3. Are leaders being held accountable for quality measures and are they rewarded when improvements have been made?
4. Have patient safety priorities been delineated for your organization?
5. Are there programs in place to develop leaders and staff in quality improvement?
6. Is leadership actively engaged in the organization's quality improvement strategy?
7. Are there specific interventions in place to improve the reliability of the system such as simplifying work processes, daily check-ins, huddles, and executive rounds?
8. Do you expect leadership to possess the same experience and expertise in quality as compared to finance?
9. Do you hold leadership accountable for quality performance at the same level as financial performance?

Index

Authors

MAULIK S. JOSHI, DrPH

Maulik S. Joshi, DrPH, is president of the Health Research and Educational Trust and senior vice president of research at the American Hospital Association. Dr. Joshi was previously the president and chief executive officer of the Network for Regional Healthcare Improvement (NRHI), the mission of which is to accelerate the improvement of the value (quality and cost) of healthcare delivery in the United States by building and strengthening regional, multistakeholder coalitions and influencing national policy for regional coalitions. Dr. Joshi has also served as a senior advisor for the Office of the Director for the Agency for Healthcare Research and Quality (AHRQ) and previously as the president and chief executive officer of the Delmarva Foundation. During his tenure at the Delmarva Foundation, the organization was the recipient of the 2005 U.S. Senate Productivity award, the highest-level award in the state of Maryland, on the basis of the national Malcolm Baldrige criteria for performance excellence. Prior to the Delmarva Foundation, Dr. Joshi was vice president of the Institute for Healthcare Improvement (IHI), co-founder and executive vice president of DoctorQuality, senior director of quality for the University of Pennsylvania Health System, and executive vice president of The HMO Group.

Dr. Joshi has a DrPH and a MHSA from the University of Michigan and a BS in Mathematics from Lafayette College. Dr. Joshi is co-editor of *The Healthcare Quality Book: Vision, Strategy and Tools*, a graduate-level textbook (Health Administration Press, second edition published in 2008).

Dr. Joshi serves on multiple organizational governance or advisory boards, including being a member of the Board of Trustees Quality and Patient Safety Committee for Catholic Healthcare Partners, the Holy Cross Health System Board of Trustees Quality Committee, the Board of Governors for the National Patient Safety Foundation, the Lafayette College Leadership Council; treasurer of the Board of Trustees for the

Center for the Advancement of Health; and secretary of the Board of Trustees for The Country School.

Dr. Joshi was selected as one of the "Healthcare Up and Comers" by Witt/Kieffer and *Modern Healthcare*; one of Philadelphia's outstanding "40 Under 40" leaders by the *Philadelphia Business Journal* for commitment to professional excellence and contributions to the community; and as one of the "21 Voices for Quality for the 21st Century" by the American Society for Quality.

BERNARD J. HORAK, PhD

Dr. Horak has a PhD from The George Washington University with specialties in health services administration and organization behavior and development. He also has a MHA in hospital administration from Baylor University, a MS in systems management from the University of Southern California, and a BS in business administration and sociology from Trinity University.

Dr. Horak is a professor and director of the Graduate Program in Health Systems Administration at Georgetown University where he also teaches courses in quality improvement, strategic planning, and organizational behavior. Dr. Horak was director of Strategic Planning and Total Quality Management at Walter Reed Army Medical Center. He has held other positions including that of chief operating officer, associate administrator for Clinical Services, and administrator of a family practice clinic.

Dr. Horak has also been a consultant in the areas of patient safety, teambuilding, cultural change, strategic planning, worker satisfaction, leadership development, customer service, and the use of information technology to improve patient care. His clients have included Humana, the Department of Veterans Affairs, the Food and Drug Administration, the General Services Administration, The Smithsonian Institution, the DC Primary Care Association, Pfizer, Merck, Provident Bank, and the U.S. Postal Service. Internationally, he has consulted in Poland, Estonia, the Czech Republic, Slovakia, Belize, Mexico, and Saudi Arabia.

Dr. Horak has published the book entitled *Strategic Planning for Healthcare: Building a Quality-Based Plan Step by Step*, written many articles, and presented at numerous national and international conferences. Dr. Horak is a Fellow in the American College of Health Care Executives (FACHE) and a Certified Professional of Healthcare Quality (CPHQ). He was awarded the Bronze Star for his leadership of medical units during the Gulf War.